Writing Tasks

Writing Tasks

An authentic-task approach to individual writing needs

David Jolly

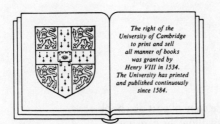

The right of the
University of Cambridge
to print and sell
all manner of books
was granted by
Henry VIII in 1534.
The University has printed
and published continuously
since 1584.

Cambridge University Press
Cambridge
New York   Port Chester
Melbourne   Sydney

Published by the Press Syndicate of the University of Cambridge
The Pitt Building, Trumpington Street, Cambridge CB2 1RP
32 East 57th Street, New York, NY 10022, USA
10 Stamford Road, Oakleigh, Melbourne 3166, Australia

© Cambridge University Press 1984

First published 1984
Sixth printing 1989

Printed in Great Britain
at The Bath Press, Avon

ISBN 0 521 22924 3 Student's Book
ISBN 0 521 28972 6 Teacher's Book

BS

Contents

Contents

Thanks

I would like to take this opportunity to thank Adrian at Cambridge University Press for encouraging the book in the first place, and my editors Christine, Kay, Geraldine and Alison, who have all been exceptionally kind and patient with me. I would also like to thank past and present colleagues and students at South Devon Technical College and Exeter College for use of and comment on the materials contained in this book. Finally, a word of quiet appreciation for all the many people I live with for tolerating a great deal of noise from a very old typewriter.

Introduction

Why this book has been written

This book has been written for foreign students of English who may need to write English now or in the near future, and have learnt enough English to be able to write complete texts fairly successfully.

This book is about writing complete texts, not just good sentences. When you have to write English for a genuine purpose you need to do more than write a lot of good English sentences; you need to write a whole text that will convey what you mean successfully.

This book therefore contains units on most of the text types that you are ever likely to need in ordinary life with the exception of commercial or technical English, for which excellent books are already available.

The Teacher's Book

The Teacher's Book contains more information on each unit and on each section. It also contains extra practice material, important exercise material for certain units (and a key for these exercises), and two tests for all the units except units 2.8 and 7.5.

If you are working in a class, your teacher will have this additional material. If you are working on your own, you will need to buy a copy of the Teacher's Book. But remember, if you do not attend English classes, you will still need a competent English-speaking person to mark your work.

How to use this book

Preparing your own programme of work

By this time in your English studies you should have a good idea of the kinds of writing that will be valuable or useful to you; it makes sense therefore to work out your own programme. Perhaps this is an unusual idea to you – perhaps you have been used to teachers suggesting what you should learn. When it comes to writing skills, however, it really makes good sense for you to think about what you need or want to write.

Below, you will find two examples of students who wrote their own programmes of work using the sections and units in this book.

Haruo   is a student studying English in his own country on a non-intensive evening institute course. When he started his course he decided that he needed to learn to write well in English, but that he wasn't all that interested in personal communication. He wanted to be able to describe, report and argue effectively. He planned his outline writing syllabus in the following way:

Writing descriptions	Units 4.1, 4.2, 4.3, 4.4, 4.6, 4.7
Reporting experiences	Units 5.1, 5.2, 5.3
Presenting facts, opinions and ideas	Units 7.1, 7.3, 7.5

Leila   is a student who has come to Britain for six months. At the moment she is at the beginning of an intensive course; she thinks that the ability to communicate personally is the most important thing for her, so she has decided that Section 1 (Writing notes and memos) and Section 2 (Writing personal letters) are the sections she should first concentrate on. She feels that parts of Section 3 (Writing telegrams etc.) and Section 6 (Writing to companies and officials) might become more important once she has been in Britain for a little while. Later on, she may decide that she needs other sorts of writing ability, but she can add other units later.

Keeping a check on your work

You should start making a note of which units you wish to work on, either on the checklist on page 6 or on a copy of it.
   Once you have made and started to use your own programme it is quite important that you (and your teacher) keep a clear record of what work you have done, are in the middle of doing, and want to do later.
   Study the checklist opposite and the notes that accompany it. This is the checklist that Haruo is using and it should give you one clear method of keeping a check on your writing work.

NOTES

Haruo is over half way through his course. If you look at the checklist opposite and the explanatory notes below, you can see how he is getting on in his writing programme. These are the conventions Haruo used:

○   Haruo put a ring round each unit he was interested in completing – he did this at the beginning of his course. Naturally, he can add more rings if he wants to do other units.

•   The dot indicates work handed to the teacher for correction, comment and advice.

Writing checklist   Student: **Mr Haruo Yakamoto**

UNIT	TITLE	STUDENT'S BOOK		TEACHER'S BOOK		
		Practice		Exercises	Extra Practice	Test
		1 2 3 4		1 2	1 2 3 4	1 2

4   Writing descriptions

- 4.1 Describing people
- 4.2 Describing places
- 4.3 Describing objects
- 4.4 Describing human scenes
- 4.5 Describing landscape
- 4.6 Describing habits and conditions
- 4.7 Describing processes

5   Reporting experiences

- 5.1 Reporting incidents and events
- 5.2 Writing biographical information
- 5.3 Narrating
- 5.4 Reporting speech

7   Presenting facts, ideas and opinions

- 7.1 Paragraph writing
- 7.2 Letters to newspapers
- 7.3 Summary reports
- 7.4 Personal and factual reports
- 7.5 Essay-writing

✓   A tick indicates a successful exercise, practice, or test.

✗   A cross indicates that the work is not good enough, and more practice needs to be done.

Practice: Some of the practices were done with other students in a small group. Haruo found this very useful, and thinks it improved the work handed in.

Tests: Haruo hasn't done many tests yet; he wants to leave them till near the end of his course. He will have to do them on his own.

Using a unit

Read these notes carefully; they will tell you how to work through a unit.

INTRODUCTIONS

Each section contains an *introduction*. Before you begin using any specific unit within a section make sure that you have read the section introduction – it may contain information or help that is applicable to all the units in that section. For example the introduction to Section 6 (Writing to companies and officials) explains how to lay out *all* letters to companies and officials.

MODELS

Each unit contains *model* texts. These include authentic English examples of the kind of text that you have decided to write. Read the models carefully and the notes that go with them. Along with the model texts you will find a section called *language notes* which should be of great help when you come to do your own writing. At the end of each model there is a set of instructions for each unit entitled *What to do*. Not all units are the same. Some units have two or three sections of practice work, in sequence. Others have alternative practices for different purposes. For an example of the kind of instructions given, see page 10.

EXERCISES

In some units it may be helpful to do some *exercises* on aspects of the language contained in the text types. For example, if you want to write good descriptions of landscape (Unit 4.5) quite a lot of special vocabulary is needed. There is exercise material for some units in the Teacher's Book. If you are working in a class, your teacher will either give you his or her own exercise material or copies of the exercises in the Teacher's Book, if you or your teacher consider this necessary.

PRACTICES

Following each model and its notes, there are *practices*. These create realistic contexts and situations in which you may practise writing whole texts.

Alone/groups: You may wish to write these practice tasks on your own; but you may prefer to work with a friend or in a group if this is possible. It can be much more fun (and also more effective!) working with other people on writing tasks than doing them entirely on your own. Don't forget that there are other sources of help when writing which might be available to you: text examples from other sources, a dictionary, your fellow students or your teacher.

Your teacher, or a competent English-speaking person, will mark your work. If your practice texts are not good enough, it is sensible to read what your teacher has corrected or written about your writing and do another practice. The idea is to go on practising until you can write good texts. If you need more practice tasks than are in the book, you can find more in the Teacher's Book.

Note: The practices in this book are all based on real-life situations which require a written communication between two English-speaking people. Therefore, it is important to remember while doing the practices, that you are writing to an *English-speaking* person or organisation. You would not, after all, write to members of your family, friends or businesses in your own country, in English. Thus, for example, when a task suggests that you write to a friend, it means an English-speaking friend.

TESTS

If your practice work is good enough (either done on your own or with somebody else) you may take a *test*. This you must do alone – just as you would probably be alone if you had to write a letter or a report in English in your own country. However, when you take a test, you should be allowed to look at the work you have already done and had marked for the unit, and also be able to use a dictionary.

If you do not write a good enough test, you should do another practice before taking a second test, even if you have already done one successful practice.

The tests are in the Teacher's Book. If you are working in a class, ask your teacher to give you a copy of the test you need.

You will find the *checklist* on the following two pages.

Writing checklist

UNIT	TITLE	STUDENT'S BOOK Practice 1 2 3 4	TEACHER'S BOOK Exercises 1 2 · Extra practice 1 2 3 4 · Test 1 2
1	**Writing notes and memos**		
1.1	Explanations		
1.2	Arrangements		
1.3	Instructions		
1.4	Inquiries and requests		
1.5	Apologies and explanations		
2	**Writing personal letters**		
2.1	Invitations		
2.2	Requests and inquiries		
2.3	Acceptances and refusals		
2.4	Arrangements		
2.5	Apologies and explanations		
2.6	Congratulations and commiserations		
2.7	Thank-you letters		
2.8	Expressing positive and negative emotions		
2.9	General personal letters		
3	**Writing telegrams, personal ads, and instructions**		
3.1	Writing telegrams and telexes		
3.2	Writing personal ads		
3.3	Writing instructions		
4	**Writing descriptions**		
4.1	Describing people		
4.2	Describing places		
4.3	Describing objects		
4.4	Describing human scenes		
4.5	Describing landscape		
4.6	Describing habits and conditions		
4.7	Describing processes		
5	**Reporting experiences**		
5.1	Reporting incidents and events		
5.2	Writing biographical information		
5.3	Narrating		
5.4	Reporting speech		

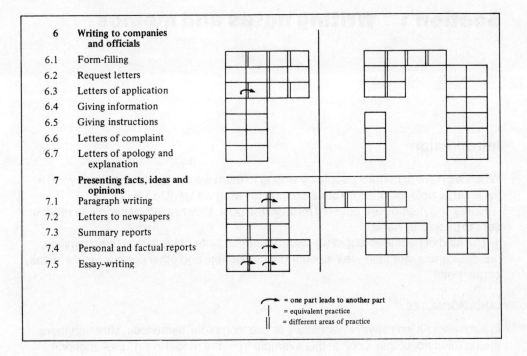

= one part leads to another part
= equivalent practice
= different areas of practice

Section 1   Writing notes and memos

Introduction

When we have to contact people by writing to them we don't always need to write a full letter; a *note* will often be quite enough for what we want to say.

Notes and memos are not sent through the post: they are *left* for people to read; or sent to people *by hand*.

The kind of people to whom we usually need to write notes are our own families, our colleagues, our flatmates, people like landladies, and other people we are in daily contact with.

LANGUAGE NOTES

In such notes it isn't always necessary to use 'complete' sentences, although there are no rules about this. Look at this example from the model in 1.1 Explanations:

>   'Key to the back door under the mat'

The writer could have written:

>   'Key to back door under mat'
> or   'The key to back door is under mat'

Address forms: You don't have to use 'dear' at the beginning (but you may do) and people do not use 'sincerely' at the end; but you must put your name on the note.

● This section covers the following areas:
1.1 Writing a note *explaining* something that's happened or is going to happen.
1.2 Writing a note *arranging* a meeting or inviting someone to something.
1.3 Leaving a note with *instructions* to do something.
1.4 Writing a note asking someone *about* something, or *for* something: *inquiries* and *requests.*
1.5 Leaving a note *apologising* for something you have or haven't done and offering an explanation for your actions.

Remember: The practices in this section are all based on real-life situations which require a written communication between two *English-speaking* people. Thus, when a task suggests that you write to a friend, acquaintance or organisation, it means an English-speaking person or organisation.

8

1.1 Explanations

Model

1 This is a note written to a friend. It has been left in the country
cottage by Avril, because her friend Jane is going to be staying there.
  Notice that some determiners (a / the / some) can be left out, and
also some of the verbs (is / are).

> Dear Jane,
>
> There's a lot of food in the fridge and milk too. Key to the back door under the mat. Hot water from immersion heater.
> If you want fresh eggs, see Ben next door.
>
> Happy stay.
>
> Love, Avril

2 George works in a library. He's written this note to Sue, a
colleague, explaining a problem about a book. Sue has just found
the note on the library desk, on top of the book in question.

> Sue
>
> Found this book on the shelves. It has the cover for Vol. 9 but the contents of Vol. 5. Have ordered both volumes again — should be here in two weeks.
>
> George

WHAT TO DO

1 Do Practice 1.
2 If you or your teacher are not satisfied with your first practice, do Practice 2. Further practice will be found on page 14 of the Teacher's Book.
3 When you are satisfied that you can write these sorts of notes well, you can take a test. This will be found on page 14 of the Teacher's Book.

Practice 1

Write both notes:

A It is Saturday afternoon, your hostess is out and you decide to go out to a nearby town; you will miss your evening meal. Write a note to your hostess explaining all this, and anything else which is important.

B Your friend lost her bag. You have just found it. Write a note to your friend explaining this, where it was found, and what you think might be missing from it. Suggest a course of action now.

Practice 2

Write both notes:

A Your English teacher has set some important homework but a fellow-student has missed the class. Write a note to him/her explaining what the homework is, why it's important, and when it has to be handed in.

B You are holding a party at your house. Friends are coming round to help you prepare for the party but you won't be there when they arrive. Explain in a note where everything for the party can be found, and what your friends can start doing.

1.2 Arrangements

Model

1 From wife to husband:

> Tony – meet you down at
> the library about 2.15 – love
> Sally

2 From friend to friend:

> Dear Jenny
>   'Star Wars' is on at Cinecentre
> 2 at 7.30. We'll meet you there
> at 7.15 for a quick coffee first.
> It'll probably go on for 2 hours.
> Pizza afterwards.
>   Alison

3 Ian Turner is going to be absent tomorrow from his office. He
wishes to put his colleague in the picture about tomorrow's office
arrangements:

> Jim   3.15pm
> (1) Mr Allen called. Wants
>   a meeting tomorrow at 11.
> (2) Forbes calling tomorrow
>   at about 3.
> (3) Remember to phone IBM.
> (4) See you first thing Thursday.
>
>   Ian Turner.

4 Sometimes arrangements are made over the phone and left in the form of a message:

> Jenny — Anne called and said she'd bring the apples over at about 9 this evening. Said no need to call back.

WHAT TO DO

1 Do Practice 1.
2 If you or your teacher are not satisfied with your first practice, do Practice 2. Further practice will be found on page 15 of the Teacher's Book.
3 When you are satisfied that you can write these sorts of notes well, you can take a test. This will be found on page 16 of the Teacher's Book.

Practice 1

Write all three notes:

A Arrange to meet a friend somewhere in town. Mention time, place, reason.

B You are alone at home when someone phones your hostess. This is what they say:

> ... oh she isn't in ... well, I wonder if you could take a message and leave it for her ... thanks ... tell her that Doreen called ... I was going to meet her at the Cadena coffee bar tomorrow at around 11, but I can't make it now – perhaps she could ring me back to arrange some other time ... got that? ... Thanks. Bye.

Now write a clear note for your hostess.

C You are working in an office in Britain, as a secretary. Tomorrow you will be away and a 'temp' will take your place. Leave her a note explaining
a) your boss's engagements
b) what must be typed/filed/who must be telephoned tomorrow.

Practice 2

Write all three notes:

A   You were going for a drink tonight with a friend. But you have
both forgotten about a programme on TV you were going to
watch. You'll have to rearrange your evening. Leave a note for
your friend suggesting a change of plan so that you may watch the
programme and have a drink (before or after).

B   Your boy/girl friend wants to go into town to buy records and get
some jeans. You also want to do two things. Suggest some
arrangements in a note to him/her.

C   You are staying in the home of a British couple. The chimney
sweep has just phoned and you answered the phone because your
host and hostess are out. The sweep wants to come and clean the
boiler chimney on 27 October. He also suggested a time when he
could come. Write your hosts a note about this telephone call.

1.3 Instructions

Model

1 Mrs Randall has asked the plumber to call today. She won't be there so she's left a list of instructions for him:

> Mr Toulson,
> Please do the following things:
> 1) Loosen air-lock in top landing radiator
> 2) Check tap washers in kitchen
> 3) Remove old pipes in small room
> 4) N.B. Leave a bill please!
>   Mrs. Randall

2 In this second note, Mrs Randall gives her husband a list of things to do:

> Mick, I won't be back till 5 so please could you do the following:
>   potatoes
>   collect bread
>   hang washing out
>   pop in next door to see if everything is OK.
>   Molly

LANGUAGE AND FORM

It helps the reader of this sort of note if you give your instructions some order with numbers (1, 2, 3 ...) or letters (a, b, c ...).
    Start instructions with the dictionary form of the verb
e.g.   1 Check ...
       2 Collect ...
       3 Hang ...

WHAT TO DO

1 Do Practice 1.
2 If you or your teacher are not satisfied with your first practice, do Practice 2.
3 When you are satisfied that you can write these sorts of notes well, you can take a test. This will be found on page 17 of the Teacher's Book.

Practice 1

Write *two* notes only:

A   You are living in a house in Britain. Write a note to the window-cleaner, instructing him which windows to clean, and which *not* to clean. Say something about payment.

B   You are staying in a friend's flat in Britain. Write a quick note to the milkman about the milk and orange juice etc. you want tomorrow.

C   You get up early to go to the city one Saturday morning. You know that your friend (who's still asleep!) is going into the centre of your local town today. Leave a list of instructions for him/her about
a)   the library
b)   the bookshop
c)   buying coffee
d)   information from travel agent's.

Practice 2

Write *two* notes:

A   You are living in a flat in Britain. Letters keep coming through your door to a person who doesn't live there any longer. Write a quick note to the postman about this, giving him an instruction.

B   You are going away on a long weekend with .... It is quite likely that at least three people will phone you, including your parents. Leave instructions with your hosts about what they are to say/do if these people call.

C   You can't get to your morning English classes one day this week. Write a quick note to a friend instructing him/her to collect exercise materials and tell the teacher(s).

1.4 Inquiries and requests

<u>*Model*</u>

1 Here is an informal request from a parent to a child. Notice the
please, but no special request formulas.

> John ———— go down to the
> corner shop when you get home
> from school, please. I want 40
> Embassy. Here is the money.
>   Mum

2 This is an inquiry followed by a request made *informally* by one
friend to another friend – the note is transmitted by hand.

> Anna – I was wondering if you still had
> two typewriters – if you have, could I
> borrow one for a few weeks, I've got lots
> of official letters to write? I'm sending
> this with Suzy – Irma

3 The next note is a formal request from a colleague to arrange an
exchange of work duties.
Notice the language used here: I wonder if ...
                                                  Would it be possible ...
                                                  I would be very grateful ...
Other possibilities: Could you possibly ...
                              I wonder if you'd mind ...
                              Would you mind in any way if ...

> Dear Alan,
>   I understand that you're on duty tomorrow night
> from 5 till midnight. I wonder if it would be possible
> for you to do my duty next Thursday night if I work
> your duty tomorrow. A friend is calling in next Thursday
> and I'd be most grateful if a swap could be arranged.
>   Robin Ford

4 The note below is an inquiry addressed to a neighbour who was out when Mrs Robertson called. Notice again the *formal* tone.

> Dear Mrs Hartop –
> would you be so kind
> as to tell me the
> names of the people
> who lived here before
> the Lindleys – someone
> has been asking about
> them. Sorry to bother
> you.
>   Mrs Robertson

WHAT TO DO

1 Do Practice 1.
2 If you or your teacher are not satisfied with your first practice, do Practice 2. Further practice will be found on page 18 of the Teacher's Book.
3 When you are satisfied that you can write these sorts of notes well, you can take a test. This will be found on page 19 of the Teacher's Book.

Practice 1

Write one *formal* and one *informal* note:

INFORMAL

A Write an informal note to a friend asking them to pick up a book from the British Council/American Information Service library, and giving the reason why you can't do this yourself.

B You are in Great Britain. Write a note to your hostess asking her permission to use the phone during the afternoon. Also ask her about the cheapest times to phone in Britain.

FORMAL

C Write a formal note to someone you don't know well (only by sight) in your place of work. You know that they're going to X at the weekend by car, and you'd like a lift there too.

D You want to borrow a typewriter from the British couple who live next door but when you call round they are out. Leave a request note for them explaining why you want to borrow the typewriter and for how long.

Practice 2

Write one *informal*, and one *formal* note:

INFORMAL

A You want to write to a London shop. You think that your friend has the address and telephone number. Write a note asking your friend for this information.

FORMAL

B You don't know your British neighbours very well, but they are at home all day. You aren't. Ask them to take in a parcel that's arriving for you tomorrow by post.

C One of your English language teachers is very interested in folk music. Leave a note in the staffroom asking for advice and help in getting some records that you want to buy but which aren't available in your local record shop.

1.5   Apologies and explanations

Model

1   A note from a student to his tutor:

> Dear David,
>   I'm afraid I can't
> be in your classes
> after coffee – my
> parents have just
> arrived. Hitoshi
> has my homework.
>   – Dani

2   A note from a colleague about a mislaid book:

> John,
>
>   Unfortunately I
> can't find your book on
> KANT – I'm sorry, it's
> probably at home – I'll
> try to bring it in
> tomorrow.
>
>   Hamish

19

3 A friend explains her lunchtime absence:

> Sorry about lunchtime, Julie :
>
> 1) My tutor caught me !
>
> 2) Someone wanted a book of mine .
>
> 3) I couldn't remember which pub you were going to.
>
> I'll make it tomorrow —
> Anne.

LANGUAGE NOTES

Making apologies: I'm (very) sorry but I . . .
I'm afraid I . . . I am sorry.

Sorry about | -ing . . .
| not -ing . . .

N.B. In *notes* you can leave out the 'I', e.g. 'Sorry about not coming on time but . . .'

WHAT TO DO

1 Do Practice 1.
2 If you or your teacher are not satisfied with your first practice, do Practice 2. Further practice will be found on page 20 of the Teacher's Book.
3 When you are satisfied that you can write these sorts of notes well, you can take a test. This will be found on page 21 of the Teacher's Book.

Practice 1

Write *two* notes:

A Write to a friend explaining your absence from a party you'd promised faithfully to go to at the weekend.

B Write to your hostess explaining how two cups came to be broken! Promise to replace them.

C Last night you walked home with an umbrella belonging to a woman who works in the same office as you, but whom you don't know well. Write her a note of apology and explanation.

It might take quite a lot of practice to get the *tone* right.

Practice 2

Write *three* notes:

A Last night you were pretty short-tempered with a good friend. Write a short note of sincere apology to him/her.

B You arranged to see one of the English teachers at 2.30 in the Institute – now you can't get there – leave him/her a note in the staffroom.

C You've forgotten to return something to a colleague, because something rather unpleasant has happened to you (personal reasons). Write a note to your colleague apologising and explaining.

D Coming in late last night to your small international hotel, you smashed a bottle of vodka in the hotel foyer. Write a note of apology and explanation at the desk, addressed to the manager.

Notes of apology are difficult to do well. Take some care with the *tone*.

Section 2   Writing personal letters

Introduction

It is not really difficult to write personal letters in English, if your purpose is quite simple. English letter-writing does not require 'flowery' language as some other languages do.

It is useful, however, to use the *form* set out below, which is how the normal personal letter is laid out:

(A) 34, Coolgardie Avenue,
Highams Park,
London E4 9HP

(B) 20 July 1984

(C) Dear Alan,
Dr/Mr/Mrs/Miss/Ms Wicks,

(D) I'm writing to you...

LETTER

(E) Love,
Yours (sincerely),

Robert (Bridge)

LANGUAGE NOTES

Ⓐ *Your* address always goes in the top right-hand corner. The address of the person you're writing to **does not appear** in a personal letter.

Ⓑ The date always goes under the address. This can be written as: Tuesday, 20th July or July 20th or 20/7/84 or 20.7.84.

Ⓒ *Dear* + *Christian name* or *Dear* + *Title* + *Surname* are the only address forms.

Ⓓ The first line of the letter usually starts below the end of the address form.

Ⓔ *Love* and variations (lots of love etc.) are intimate or affectionate; *Yours* is friendly without expressing intimacy; *Yours sincerely* is quite formal in a personal letter. There are other very personal and individual ways of ending a personal letter that you'll develop naturally with close friends.

● This section covers the following areas:

2.1 Writing letters of *invitation*.

2.2 Writing letters making *requests* to people (for goods or information) or asking for information.

2.3 Writing letters which *accept* or *refuse* invitations.

2.4 Writing letters in order to make future *arrangements* with someone.

2.5 Writing letters of *apology*.

2.6 Writing letters which *congratulate* someone for something they've done or for something good that's happened to them: writing letters which *commiserate* with someone's misfortune or unhappiness.

2.7 Writing *thank-you* letters.

Each unit in Section 2 will contain useful language notes with the model.

Two other units are available in this section:

2.8 Writing letters in which you express your *feelings and emotions*, both negative and positive emotions, such as pleasure, surprise, disappointment, irritation. Such letters are not easy to write well.

2.9 Writing letters in which you *talk about yourself, give news, give information* and tell *anecdotes* (little stories). These letters also require the ability to report and describe and are more difficult to write than the letters in units 2.1–2.7.

Remember: The practices in this section are all based on real-life situations which require written communication between two *English-speaking* people. Thus, when a task suggests that you write to a friend, acquaintance or organisation, it means an English-speaking person or organisation.

FINAL NOTE

One wouldn't always write a letter just containing an invitation or making an arrangement. By practising these things now, however, you will be able to do them in letters when you need to.

2.1 Invitations

Model

This is a letter of invitation from a man and a woman to a friend of the same age to come and stay with them.

> 26 Hope Road
> TORQUAY
> Devon TQ6 8PR
> 26 October 1984
>
> Dear Jo,
>   I've just heard from your parents that you're back in England and looking for a new job. While you're waiting, why don't you come down and see us for a few days or longer — we've got a spare room? It hasn't begun to rain yet so, with luck, we ought to be able to visit a few places in the area, even take a walk on Dartmoor.
>   Well, think about it, and we both hope you can come.
>   Love,
>   Liz (and Robert).

LANGUAGE NOTES

The expression of invitation in this letter was '... why don't you come ...'

Others are: 'How about coming ...'
        'We think it'd be a good idea if ...'

More tentative invitations would use expressions like:
  'Is there any chance of you/your coming ...'
  'We were wondering if you could/wanted to come ...'

Invitations to people of a different age or to people you don't know very well would use expressions like:
    'We would like to ask you to come ...'
    'We wondered if you'd like to come ...'
    'We would like to invite you to ...'

WHAT TO DO

1 Do Practice 1 (write *one* letter only).
2 If you or your teacher are not happy with your first practice, do Practice 2.
3 You may take a test when you and your teacher think you can write good invitation letters. Tests will be found on page 23 of the Teacher's Book.

Practice 1

Write A *or* B:

A You are having a dinner party. Invite a friend – in a letter, not a note – to the party. Give details.

B The parents of a very close friend have decided to visit your country for a holiday. You don't know them very well, but would like to offer them hospitality or your time as a guide.

Practice 2

Write A *or* B:

A You'd like to go to Yugoslavia for a holiday next summer. Write and invite a friend to go with you.

B You're going to be in London for a couple of nights. Two British friends of yours live there. Invite them out for a meal – at your expense – while you're there.

2.2 Requests and inquiries

Model

Below you'll find a letter from a girl in Wales to a friend in London.
She wants to spend a few days in London.

10, Grange Avenue,
Chepstow,
Wales CH5 3NA

1/2/84

Dear Ali,

     I'm thinking about killing two birds with one stone. The stone is a three-day trip to London from Friday 10th of March till the Monday. The birds are seeing all those films I've wanted to see but can't in Chepstow, and seeing you.

Would it be possible, Ali, to stay in your flat for that weekend, with you — or, if you're away — without you — which would be a pity, but still convenient. Of course, I'd like very much to see you, and this seems a marvellous opportunity if you're going to be there.

Please could you let me know at once so that if it's not possible, I could make other arrangements......

LANGUAGE NOTES

Request language

polite forms:	Would it be possible to .../for you to ...
	Please could I ... (possibly)
	Please could you ...
formal forms:	I'd be most/very grateful if you'd / I could ...
informal forms:	Can I / could I ...
hesitant forms:	Is there any chance of me/my coming to stay ...
	I was wondering if I could / you could / would ...

Inquiry language (this can use rather similar forms)
I wonder if you could tell me ...
Would it be possible to ... (something general)
I'd like to know if ...
Do you happen to know if ...
Can you remember whether ... (informal)

WHAT TO DO

1 Do Practice 1 (write *both* letters).
2 If you or your teacher are not happy with your first practice, do
  Practice 2. Further practice will be found on page 25 of the
  Teacher's Book.
3 You may take a test when you and your teacher think you can
  write good letters of request and inquiry. Tests will be found on
  page 25 of the Teacher's Book.

Practice 1

Write a letter of request and a letter of inquiry:

REQUEST

A You are back in your own country after spending some time with a
  British family. You would like to stay with them again in July.
  Write a letter to the family, requesting this.

INQUIRY

B You've returned to your own country and you suddenly need to
  know – in some detail – something about English newspapers.
  Write to a friend and ask him for the information.

Practice 2

Write either A and B (two letters) or C (one combined letter):

REQUEST

A Write to a friend asking him/her to send you four books – mention
  money (payment) etc.

INQUIRY

B Write to your former English teacher asking him what books you
  should study and things you should do, now that you've finished
  your course in Britain and want to go on improving your English.

REQUEST AND INQUIRY

C You left Britain in a great hurry and left lots of things in the flat of
  a friend. Now you'd like the friend to send them to you. You'd
  also like to know about work permits and residence permits in Britain.
  Write to your friend requesting your things and inquiring about permits.

2.3 Acceptances and refusals

Model

If you can't, or prefer not to, thank someone in person or over the phone, for an invitation or offer, then it will be necessary to write a letter, either accepting or refusing. Such letters are quite simple to write, and can be quite short. (N.B. not too short, however, or they will seem impolite!)

1 *Acceptance*
   Renata's former landlady (in Bristol) has asked Renata to come from Warwick for the weekend, for a party on Saturday night. This is Renata's reply:

> 10, Castle Lane,
> Warwick CV14 3BZ
> June 8th
>
> Dear Sybil,
>   It was very nice to get your invitation to spend the weekend after next with you – luckily I'm completely free then, so I'll say 'yes' – and I'll be arriving in Bristol at around 9 p.m. on Friday evening. The idea of a party on Saturday sounds marvellous and I promise to bring you a cake for it – a German speciality! Well, see you then,
>   Love,
>   Renata

LANGUAGE NOTES (ACCEPTANCE)

I'd be	very pleased delighted very happy	to	come to ... accept your ...

Your invitation to ...	is very welcome was a delightful/lovely surprise ...

Thank you / Thanks for your ... The answer is 'yes' ...

2 *Refusal*

Michael has been invited to the wedding in Holland of a Dutch
friend. Unfortunately his work commitments make it impossible
for him to go to his friend's wedding. Here is his polite refusal.

'Leyden'
Brigg Terrace,
Colchester
Essex CO5 4NZ
25th October

Dear Margarita,
Thank you for your invitation to
your wedding at the beginning of December —
I was pleased to learn that you and Franz
have decided on 'something' at last.
Unfortunately, much as I'd like to be at the
wedding, especially a Dutch wedding (!), it
simply isn't possible for me to take that
weekend off; I have to work fairly late
on Friday night, and friends are coming
down to stay from Sunday lunchtime
so there would be no way in which I
could squeeze a wedding in Holland in
between.
So all I can do is to wish you the
happiest of days and also of futures.
Love, Michael

LANGUAGE NOTES (REFUSAL)

informal: I'm (very) sorry but | I'll have to refuse . . . / say 'no' . . .
| I simply can't make it . . . / come . . .

I'm terribly sorry to have to . . .

a little more formal: Thank you for your . . . but unfortunately . . .
It's not possible for me to . . . / (quite) impossible
for me to . . .
I'm quite unable to . . .

N.B. When you refuse an invitation, offer, or request always give a
convincing explanation for your refusal. If you don't, your
letter will sound very impolite.

29

WHAT TO DO

1 Do Practice 1 (write *two* letters).
2 If you or your teacher are not happy with your first practice, do Practice 2.
3 You may take a test when you and your teacher think you can write good letters of acceptance and refusal. Tests will be found on page 26 of the Teacher's Book.

Practice 1

There are three situations below. Write *two* letters; an acceptance for one situation and a refusal for another:

A A friend, living in a different town in Britain from you, has written to you, inviting you to go for a week's holiday in Wales at Easter. Accept or refuse this invitation.

B A group of people from Britain are coming to your town to visit various places of interest. As they do not speak your language, an acquaintance of yours in the British Council has written to you informally asking you to be an interpreter for two days for this group. Write a letter refusing or accepting this request.

C Before you left Britain, you and a friend spent a day looking round second-hand shops for a complete edition of Dickens/Shakespeare/Scott. This friend has now written to you saying she's found what you wanted. Write a suitable letter back either asking her to buy it for you or saying that you don't think it's quite what you wanted, giving reasons.

Practice 2

There are three situations below. Write *two* letters; an acceptance for one situation and a refusal for another:

A Friends of your hostess whom you've got to know in the last few weeks have invited you to dinner next Friday evening. Accept or refuse this invitation.

B A girl you know has written offering you a ticket to Shakespeare's *The Tempest* next Friday evening. Write a letter of acceptance or refusal.

C A former colleague has written to you from another town in your country and has asked you to spend the weekend with him/her and his/her family. Write a letter of acceptance or refusal.

2.4 Arrangements

Model

Derek Martin is planning to visit some German friends who live in Hamburg.
This is the letter he wrote to them telling them of his arrangements.

> 12 Uverdale Road
> London SW7
>
> May 14th.
>
> Dear Ulrich and Berthe,
>
> I thought I'd drop you a line to confirm the arrangements for my trip over to Germany – I must say, I'm really looking forward to it.
>
> I should be leaving Heathrow Airport at 10 in the morning of the 27th. The flight gets in at half-past eleven or thereabouts. Could you meet me at the airport? I'd like to stay with you for three days, and then, on the 31st of May, I'm going across the border to Koge in Denmark to see another old friend for a couple of days. I'll be back with you on about the 3rd of June and then we can go off on our travels through southern Germany. I must be back in England on the 18th of June.
>
> I hope these arrangements are OK with you. Till then ...
>
> Yours Derek

LANGUAGE NOTES

Your arrangements: I'll be leaving/arriving ...
                             I should be getting in at about 6.
Your plans and proposals: I'm spending ...
                                 I'm going to spend ...
                                 I've arranged to ...
                                 I'm planning to ...
                                 I'm thinking of ...
Transport timetables: It gets in at ...
                                 The flight leaves at ...
Hopes and desires: I'm hoping to ...
                             I'd like to / I want to ...
                             One thing I'd like to do ... / to arrange is to ...

WHAT TO DO

1 Do Practice 1 (write *one* letter only).
2 If you or your teacher are not happy with your first practice, do Practice 2. Further practice will be found on page 27 of the Teacher's Book.
3 You may take a test when you and your teacher think you can write good letters for making arrangements. Tests will be found on page 28 of the Teacher's Book.

Practice 1

Write *one* letter:

A In a couple of weeks you are going to stay with an American family in New England. Write a letter to them confirming the details of your arrival and explaining your travel needs in New England.

B Some people you met once at an international conference are going to have a reunion party. Write to one of these people suggesting some clear party arrangements for:
    where
    when
    kind of party
    food and drink
    organisation

Practice 2

Write *one* letter:

A A long time ago, you discussed a trip through the United States/ South America with a friend. This is now possible for both of you. Write a letter to your friend suggesting a route and a timetable.

B You had to return to your own country very quickly and you've left a lot of things in a mess in Britain. Write to a friend / your school or place of work / your host family, and suggest suitable arrangements for:
    your car
    your clothes and books
    the cancellation of a trip to Wales
    your probable (but much later) return

2.5 Apologies and explanations

Model

When you need to write a letter of apology, it is clear that explanation
is also required. Below you can read a letter from someone
apologising for not coming to see a friend in Greece, and giving
explanations for this failure.

```
                                    18 The Warren
                                    Stoke Gabriel
                                    Devon EX15 1LM

                                    December 22nd 1984



Dear Chryssoula,
              I'm terribly sorry that I failed to arrive
in Athens last Friday. I hope that this did not mess you
up completely, although I know that you had already made
some special arrangements for my visit with your parents
and friends. I'm very sorry about all that. I'm sure you'll
be sympathetic, however, when I tell you that my father is
dangerously ill in a London hospital, and that I found it
impossible to leave England when he is in this state.
```

LANGUAGE NOTES

There are a number of simple phrases that could be useful in
expressing apology:
I must apologise for -ing . . .
I do apologise for -ing . . .

I'm | awfully / terribly | sorry | about -ing . . . / for -ing . . . (more informal)

However, when it comes to expressing personal emotions, the tone in
which you do so is very important. The learning of a few phrases will
not be sufficient to guarantee a sincere-sounding apology. The person
who marks your work will give you advice on this.

WHAT TO DO:

1 Do Practice 1 (write *one* letter only).
2 If you or your teacher are not happy with your first practice, do Practice 2. Further practice will be found on page 29 of the Teacher's Book
3 You may take a test when you and your teacher think you can write good, sincere letters of apology. Tests will be found on page 30 of the Teacher's Book.

Practice 1

Write *one* of the following letters:

A You had to leave Britain and your friends in a great hurry. Write a letter to one of your friends, or colleagues, apologising for leaving without saying goodbye, and explaining why.

B For some time you've been seeing a lot of an attractive man/girl – your common language is English. You feel, however, that since he/she is returning to his/her own country soon this friendship must come to an end (i.e. you want to end the relationship!). Write a letter explaining this.

Practice 2

Write *one* of the following letters:

A A friend came to stay with you for about a week, a little while ago. You feel that you didn't give him/her as much attention as you should have done. Apologise for this and explain why it happened (personal reasons/problems).

B You had promised an acquaintance that you would send him/her .... Now, for some reason or other, you find you can't. Explain and apologise.

2.6 Congratulations and commiserations

Model

1 We write letters of *congratulation* to people – friends, family,
close acquaintances – when something pleasant happens to them,
or they are successful in something. Below is a short letter
congratulating someone on deciding to get married.

35A The Close
York YK1 8PL

June 10th

Dear Jack

Great and surprising news — congratulations on your decision to drop the cynical pose and become 'a married man'. Seriously though, I'm delighted that you and Lucy have decided to get married, and I hope that you both stay delighted with the idea.

Chris

LANGUAGE NOTES

It is impossible to suggest rules for the language used to express
congratulation but the following could be used:
formal: I congratulate you on -ing ...
neutral: I'm delighted/pleased to hear that you ...
informal: It was great to hear that you ...

Congratulations on | -ing ...
| your success in -ing ...

casual: Well done!

2 The second letter is written after an unhappy event – a death.
   Letters of *commiseration* are quite difficult to write with sincerity.

'Oaklands' 8, Cromer Way, Sheringham, Norfolk NR4 7BY

May 28th.

Dear, dear Bernadette,
                        I was very sorry
to hear of the death of your mother -
especially since I know how close you
were to her. It must be a very distressing
time for you, Emma, and your father - if
I can do anything, please don't hesitate
to contact me,
                        love, John.

LANGUAGE NOTES

Making language suggestions about how to express sympathy may
seem somewhat impertinent, but these expressions are available to
writers of English:
formal: I commiserate with you ...
neutral: I was | very sorry to hear that ...
              | deeply upset to learn that ...
        I send you my (heartfelt) sympathies/sympathy ...
offers of help: If I can | do anything | don't hesitate to let
                          | be of any help | me know.

WHAT TO DO:

1 Do Practice 1 (write one letter from A, congratulating, and one
   from B, commiserating).
2 If you or your teacher do not feel satisfied that you can write these
   letters well, do Practice 2, but only repeat the writing practice in
   the section you didn't do well in (A or B). Further practice will be
   found on page 31 of the Teacher's Book.
3 You may take a test when you or your teacher feel that you write
   letters that congratulate or commiserate well. Tests will be found
   on page 32 of the Teacher's Book.

Practice 1

CONGRATULATION

A Write to *one* of these people:

i) Your friend's daughter – she's just had her first baby.

ii) A friend of yours who has just written to tell you that he's/she's engaged to someone from your country.

COMMISERATION

B Write to *one* of the following people:

i) A friend whose marriage has just broken up.

ii) One of your colleagues whose child was injured in a road accident a little while ago.

Practice 2

CONGRATULATION

A Write a letter to *one* of these people:

i) A friend who has just got a job in Brazil.

ii) An acquaintance who has just got a job in your country.

COMMISERATION

B Write a letter to *one* of these people:

i) Your colleague who has just broken a leg and is in hospital.

ii) A young friend who has just been in a nasty car accident.

2.7 Thank-you letters

Model

The thank-you letter is most common after Christmas! But people often need to – and often want to – write letters expressing gratitude: for services, for presents, for kindnesses, for contact. Below you'll find a letter thanking someone for showing courtesy on a professional visit.

The Metallurgy Dept,
UNIVERSITY OF LIVERPOOL
Liverpool LR5 6K1
England
                              15.11.83

Dear Mr Hallinen,

          I must write and
thank you for your kindness to me
personally on my visit to the
Tampella factory earlier this month.
I am very grateful for the time you
spent answering my somewhat
persistent questions, and the trouble
you went to, to make my stay in
Tampere as interesting as possible.
In fact, I can assure you those two
days were the highlight of my trip to
Finland.

          Yours very sincerely,

          G. R. Finlay

          George R. Finlay

LANGUAGE NOTES

Some expressions of gratitude:

neutral: Thank you very much for   -ing ...
          I must thank you for ...

more formal: I am | extremely grateful ... | for   your help ...
                   | most grateful ... | showing me ...

informal: Thanks (enormously) for ...
           It was very good/nice of you to ...

WHAT TO DO

1 Do Practice 1 (write *one* letter only).
2 If you or your teacher are not happy with your first practice, do
   Practice 2.
3 You may take a test when you and your teacher think you can
   write good thank-you letters. Tests will be found on page 33 of the
   Teacher's Book.

Practice 1

Write the following letter to your host family upon your return to
your own country:

A thank-you letter for hospitality, attention shown to you, and
particular memories.

Practice 2

Write *one* of the following thank-you letters:

A You've just been on a week's holiday with a family you've known
   since your teens. Write and thank them for the holiday, in your
   shared language, English.

B A boy/girl has just sent you a present on your birthday – it's
   something that he/she remembers that you said you liked. Write a
   sincere thank-you letter.

2.8 Expressing positive and negative emotions

Model

1 You may wish at some time to express *positive* emotions:
happiness, love, delight, amazement, surprise and so on, in English.
It is almost impossible to give 'models' of such writing, since the
form of the letter depends so much on the emotional content.

    However, read the extract from the letter below:

```
and I must confess I never expected to be so charmed by
Rolf - I didn't meet him before Lynn's marriage to him -
but he's very charming and cultivated. In fact the whole
family have been very sweet. It's so lovely to see Lynn
so happy and looking so 'green and fresh', as if life is
all cream and roses. The house here is rather sweet, too -
small but warm and cosy, with a log-fire burning permanently
in the old grate. The furniture is all glossy mahogany.
Actually I find the house a bit over-heated, but who cares
when the company is so convivial.
    One nice thing about being here is that people tend to
be very active on Sundays! Up early, boots on, wind-jackets
too, and off into the mountains; on top of the mountain, to
my amazement and delight, there are wooden 'pubs' serving
```

Expressing your emotions adequately is difficult and your teacher will
try to help you choose the right sort of words and expressions to do
this. However, they are *your* emotions and so tonal correction can be
difficult.

LANGUAGE NOTES

It's impossible to do more than suggest a few ideas:

love: I've fallen in love / I'm head-over-heels in love ...
      I'm becoming very fond of / attached to ...
      I feel very/absolutely ...

delight: I'm delighted/amazed/overwhelmed ...

Essentially you should learn how *you* best express your emotions in
English, and not rely too much on standard expressions. Such letters
are usually very close to speech – more 'formal' language tends to
dilute the expressed emotions.

2 You may need to express *negative* emotions: anger, irritation, depression, disappointment, fear, worry and so on.

Read this extract from a letter by someone who is both irritated and depressed by a personal situation involving friends:

```
and when I got back I felt depressed about

the whole ghastly situation.  I hate the way

Chris and Susi just refuse to talk to each other

- it has an awful effect on the children.  I know

these days this sort of break-up is common, but

being so close to it makes me feel very

miserable.  There's a sinking, empty feeling in

the stomach as you realise that a part of young

life is being destroyed.  Actually, I get very

angry just talking to Chris but I don't think that

really helps anyone.
```

LANGUAGE NOTES

A few more ideas:

anger: I was furious / very irritated / extremely angry ...
       ... it really irritates/infuriates me ...
       I'm sick and tired of ...
       I can't stand / can't bear ...

depression: I'm not exactly full of the joys of spring ...
       I'm fed up (with) ...
       I'm feeling ... unhappy/depressed/miserable ...

disappointment: I was hoping/expecting to ... but (sadly/
       unfortunately) ...

fear/worry: I'm rather worried/afraid/frightened (that) (of) ...
       I'm terrified ... scared ...

However, this list is only an indication of some of the ways negative emotions may be expressed.

WHAT TO DO

1 Do Practice 1 (write one letter from A, positive, and one from B, negative).
2 If you or your teacher do not feel satisfied that you can write positive and negative letters well, do Practice 2, but only repeat the writing practice in the section you didn't do well in (A or B). Further practice will be found on page 34 of the Teacher's Book.
3 There are no tests for this unit.

Practice 1

Write *two* letters, one expressing positive emotions and one expressing negative emotions:

A POSITIVE

   i) You've been out of your country for some time and now you're back home. Write a letter to a friend saying how delighted you are to be home again, back among friends, and familiar things.

   ii) You are slightly surprised and certainly delighted to have (a) got a place at a university faculty or (b) been given new and exciting responsibilities in your job. Write to a friend, expressing your delight and your hopes for the future.

B NEGATIVE

   i) A friend in your country suggested a holiday in the English Midlands. You took his/her advice but the holiday so far has been very disappointing, and occasionally a little unpleasant. Write an aggrieved letter to this acquaintance.

   ii) You've just had a monumental row with your boy/girl friend and you're feeling very depressed. Write a letter to a friend to let your feelings out!

Practice 2

Write *two* letters, one expressing positive emotions, and one negative emotions:

A POSITIVE

    i) You've just met a delightful British person in X and you're fascinated with him/her. Write to a friend about this person.

    ii) When you came to London or another British city you weren't expecting to be impressed, but you are now! You like almost everything in the place! Write an enthusiastic letter back to a British friend in your own country.

B NEGATIVE

    i) There's been a death in your family recently, and also serious illness. These problems have rather depressed you. Write to a friend, in the hope of a cheering letter back.

    ii) You used to live, very happily, with an American girl in a London flat. You're now sharing a flat with two people in another town in Britain, and they have begun to irritate you in a very serious way. Write to your American friend expressing your irritation.

2.9   General personal letters

<u>*Model*</u>

We tend to write such letters to people we get on quite well with, and they are ways of keeping in touch, by communicating bits of news, information, and personal anecdotes. No two letters of this sort are ever the same (one may be light and gossipy, another serious and thoughtful) but the style of such letters is usually very close to the idioms and 'feel' of speech.

Read this letter from an English man to a Finnish friend:

```
                              The Lodge
                              Mansell Avenue
                              Leeds
                              Yorkshire
                              LS6 5AL

                              August 8th. 1983

Dear Tapio,
          I have an evening stretched out before me,
so I thought that a good way of filling it up would
be to tell you about things here. The first thing -
perhaps you saw it in the Finnish newspapers - is that
Leeds have been losing all their football matches, and
everyone's a bit fed up about that. Their new manager
has just gone and left too; he was only there for four
weeks! Bob and I are probably going to stop going
along - it's all getting too much.
     Actually, I'm also a bit frightened. Last time we
went it was a game against Manchester City. A lot of
their fans had come over the night before and by the
time they got into the ground they were pretty drunk.
I was unlucky enough to be squeezed in the corner of
the terraces surrounded by a load of City fans - well,
Leeds scored the first goal and I started jumping up
and down, it was a pretty good goal, and then three
large Manchester people jumped on me. Fortunately
three even larger Leeds policemen happened to be
standing quite near and they got me out before I'd
lost all my teeth. Actually, we lost that game...So
you can see why I'm not too enchanted about going
back again yet.
     I hope life is still treating you well. You mentioned
```

Such letters tend to include:

Ⓐ Descriptions and remarks about present conditions/circumstances
(Leeds have been losing . . . it's all getting too much.)

Ⓑ Anecdotes and things that have happened to the writer (A lot of their
   fans had come over ... they got me out before I'd lost all my teeth.)
Ⓒ Comments upon life/events (I'm a bit frightened ...).
Ⓓ Inquiries about personal health and happiness.

WHAT TO DO

1 Do Practice 1.
2 If you or your teacher are not happy with your first practice do
  Practice 2. Further practice will be found on page 36 of the
  Teacher's Book.
3 You may take a test when you and your teacher think you can
  write good, interesting personal letters. Tests will be found on page
  36 of the Teacher's Book.

Practice 1

Imagine that you are in your own country, and writing to an
English-speaking friend anywhere in the world.

Include the following things:
a) Say something about your health and ask about your friend's.
b) Information about your brother/sister, who is known to the
   person you're writing to.
c) Describe the events surrounding a big argument with your boss.
   Comment.
d) In the last letter you got your friend was a bit upset about a small fire
   he/she had had in the flat he/she lives in. Say something about this.
e) Say something about your flat.

Practice 2

Imagine that you're having a lazy holiday somewhere on the
Mediterranean. Write a letter to a friend in Britain.

Do the following things:
a) Describe and comment on the weather, and ask about the weather
   where your friend lives.
b) Talk about the kind of day you usually have on holiday.
c) One day you lost all your money – and, amazingly enough, found
   it again. Tell your friend about this incident.
d) Your friend's last letter described a rather unhappy experience
   with his/her parents. Comment upon this and perhaps say
   something you think might be helpful.
e) Comment upon some of the other people in the hotel.

Section 3 Writing telegrams, personal ads and instructions

Introduction

Some writing has to be very short
– either because it concerns something very practical where length is inconvenient (on maps, labelled diagrams, instructions etc.)
– or because using a lot of words costs money (as in telegrams, telexes, and advertising)!
 The skills needed in this kind of writing are those that involve being able to leave things out without obscuring the meaning. So you must find out what you can leave out in English without making the meaning impossible to understand.

LANGUAGE NOTES

In English you can often (but *not* always) leave out the following kinds of words:

a/the/some/any	(The) postman brought (a) letter.
is/have	Ian (is) here. / Robin (has) been skiing.
I/he/she	(I) arrived back yesterday.
my/his/our	Bring (your) camera with you.
in/on/at	Mike (at) home now. / Parcel came (on) Monday.

If you need to reduce the number of words used (as in telegrams particularly) you should look for neater ways of saying something. 'I'm returning home at about six o'clock' becomes 'Back around 6'.

● This section covers the following areas:
3.1 Writing *telegrams* or *telexes* of request, responses to requests, plans and arrangements, information-giving, congratulation and commiseration.
3.2 Writing *personal advertisements* (small ads) to put into newspapers when you want to buy or sell, get a job, find a place to live.
3.3 Writing *instructions*, including labelled maps, cookery recipes, procedures, and technical instructions.

Remember: The practices in this section are all based on real-life situations which require a written communication between two *English-speaking* people. Thus, when a task suggests that you write to a friend, acquaintance or organisation, it means an English-speaking person or organisation.

N.B. This section is of most use to people who intend to live in Britain (or another English-speaking country) for some time or who are preparing for an examination.

3.1 Writing telegrams and telexes

Model

Words cost money when you write telegrams, so the secret of writing
telegrams is to say precisely what you want to say in as few words as
possible.

When you write telegrams, then, you are allowed to leave out
determiners (a/the/some etc.) parts of verbs (am/have etc.) and
prepositions (in/at etc.) as long as your meaning remains clear.

1 Requests

```
ALL MONEY STOLEN SEND FIFTY POUNDS IMMEDIATELY CARE
YOUTH HOSTEL ATHENS PETER
```

2 Response to requests

```
FIFTY POUNDS ARRIVING CENTRAL LLOYDS BANK ATHENS
WEDNESDAY STOP MORE NEEDED INFORM FATHER
```

3 Plans and arrangements

```
UNABLE ARRIVE TUESDAY NIGHT STOP MEETING WEDNESDAY
STOP ARRIVING FRIDAY MORNING GATWICK WITH BETH
GEORGE
```

4 Information: positive

```
DON'T FAINT STOP GOT MARRIED YESTERDAY IN NEWCASTLE
STOP CROSS FINGERS STOP LINDY PAUL
```

5 Information: negative

```
JOHN KILLED LAST NIGHT ACCIDENT CAN YOU COME
IMMEDIATELY STOP NATALIE NEEDS YOU BOTH RICHARD
```

6 Congratulation or commiseration

```
TOUGH LUCK MAGGIE FRENCH JOB WHY NOT TRY FOREIGN
OFFICE STOP COME DOWN NEXT WEEKEND STOP JO
```

WHAT TO DO

1 Look at the model telegrams and read the simple language notes.
2 If you would like to practise making English sentences shorter, ask your teacher to give you the exercise materials for Unit 3.1 on page 39 of the Teacher's Book. The key to those exercises is on page 152 of the Teacher's Book.
3 Do Practice 1. If you find this difficult, do Practice 2. Extra practice can be found on page 40 of the Teacher's Book.
4 When you think you can do this kind of writing well, take a test (page 40 of the Teacher's Book).

Practice 1

Write *four* of the following telegrams:

A To a friend: you left your driving-licence in his house by mistake. You need it urgently.

B To a close friend abroad: acknowledge the receipt of a big parcel which arrived 15 minutes ago.

C To a landlady: give details of your arrival in Britain, and your requirements for transport.

D To a friend: you're happy as you've just heard about an interesting job you've been offered in London starting next week.

E To the parents of a British friend: your friend has just been taken off by the police for a motoring/currency/political offence in your country.

F To an old boy/girl friend of yours: he/she is getting married next week.

Practice 2

Write *four* of the following telegrams:

A To a British company: you work for a firm in your country which
   is expecting some goods from the company that have not arrived.
   Request an explanation.

B To the woman you are going to work for as an au pair: you must
   change your arrangements with her quickly.

C To a friend: your friend is waiting to hear whether/when you're
   coming to start a holiday in Britain with him/her. But your mother
   is ill. Send a telegram.

D To your in-laws: announce the birth of your first child.

E To a customer: you work in a record shop in your country – reply
   to a request from a British person.

F To a friend: she has just got a divorce.

3.2   Writing personal ads

Model

People sometimes find it necessary to place advertisements in the local or even the national newspapers. These advertisements (small ads) cost so much *per line* – to be brief and concise is financially important!

1   Births, Deaths, Marriages, Memorials.

BIRTHS

LAMBERT. — On Oct. 7, 1982, at St Mary's Hospital, Manchester, to JENNIFER and ROGER. A Daughter (Harriet Jennifer), a Sister for Alex.

MARRIAGES

JOHNSON—PITCHER. — On Oct 25, 1982, at Beverley Humberside, RICHARD JOHNSON, only Son of Philip and Esther Johnson, of Thorpe Market, Norwich, to CAROLINE PITCHER, only Daughter of Mr and Mrs W. Pitcher, of Hessle, Humberside.

DEATHS

TICKELL (ANNE). — On Oct. 29, 1982, late of 2 Midhurst Road, Benton, Anne, beloved Wife of Alan, dear Mother of Paul, Stephen and Robert. Service at Benton Methodist Church, on Thursday, November 4, at 2.20 p.m., followed by private cremation. Family flowers only, but donations, if desired, to St Oswald's Hospice Development Appeal, Mea House, Ellison Place, Newcastle Upon Tyne NE1 8XS.

IN MEMORIAM

BULLOUGH.—In loving memory of FLORENCE M. BULLOUGH, the beloved wife of the late Percy, and darling mother of Joan, September 19. 1973. 26 Seabourne Road, Holyhead.

2   Things you want to *buy* (wanted) or *sell* (for sale).

Articles Wanted

WANTED. Encyclopaedia Britannica, 15th edition, also children's 3rd edition. — (05086) 2839.
WANTED TOYS, Lego, Playpeople, large Fisher Price, toy hoover, action man and sindy dolls and accessories. Must be good condition. Tel. Crafts Hill 81363   4/85C

SECONDHAND furniture, old-fashioned / modern / complete houses. Bought for cash. — Cooper's, 211 / 213 Newmarket Road, Cambridge. Tel: 350065.
SINCLAIR ZX81. preferably with 16K ram. — Ely 721516.

Articles for Sale

GARDEN pool, fibreglass, £50 ono. Gas fire, Cannon Icebreaker, £50 ono. — Haverhill 704837.
KNEEHOLE desk, good condition, £25, dining hatch, wood frame, sliding glass doors, £5, strong workbench, £5. — Royston 43980.
LOGS for sale, 3 cubic yards, £27.50. 6 cubic yards, £50. — Lacer Ltd, Earith. Phone: Ramsey 840086 or 841033.

3   A place to live (accommodation wanted).

ACCOMMODATION WANTED

SMALL UNFURNISHED FLAT required for middle aged gentleman. Must be permanent. References supplied. — Telephone Torquay 63733 day, or 65463 evenings.   225x
TWO / THREE Bedroomed House or Flat, Ellacombe area. Business person, excellent references. — Torquay 23445.   225p

PERMANENT FURNISHED OR UNFURNISHED FLAT required. 1/2 bedrooms, references available. — Mrs Bond, 20 Cambridge Street, Carlton, Notts.   p
TEMPORARY PAIGNTON HOUSE/BUNGALOW from Sept. 30th for three adults, whilst seeking new property. — Paignton 550682.

4 A job you need (situation wanted).

```
┌─────────────────────────┐
│  SITUATIONS WANTED      │
└─────────────────────────┘
```
FULLY-TRAINED and experienced chef looking
for work Corby area immediately. Phone Corby
665731

WHAT TO DO

1 Read the model small ads very carefully, and make sure you
   understand them all. If necessary, ask your teacher for help.
2 Do Practice 1. If your first practice isn't good enough, do Practice 2.
3 Tests for this unit can be found on page 42 of the Teacher's Book.

Practice 1

Write *three* small ads from this list, to be placed in a local British newspaper:

A You want to buy an English language dictionary.

B You want to sell your car (cost/type/condition).

C You're looking for a flat in the town (area/price etc.).

D You want a job as an au pair locally (when / how long for etc.).

E You're looking for a lift to Scotland, in the middle of December
   from a town in England.

Practice 2

Write *three* small ads from this list, to be placed in a local British newspaper.

A You're in need of a bike (condition/price).

B You want to get rid of a tape-recorder you no longer use
   (make/price/age).

C You are going to spend six months in London – you don't have
   anywhere to live yet (when/where/size).

D You have a flat and you're looking for someone to share it
   (sex/size/time etc.).

E You want to stay in England – you want/need a summer job
   (precisely when/type/where/duration).

51

3.3 Writing instructions

Model

When you write instructions of any sort you must combine accuracy of detail with brevity and order. Look at the language notes below; they should be very valuable aids to writing clear, concise instructions.

1 Recipes

STEWED IN A PAN
1 lb. young rhubarb, 4 oz. granulated
sugar, to taste, ½ pint water.
Wash, trim and cut rhubarb into short lengths. Dissolve sugar in the water over a low heat. Add the rhubarb and bring, very slowly, up to simmering point. It should be tender but whole.

CASSEROLED
1 lb. rhubarb, 2 tablespoons
water, 4 oz. granulated sugar,
to taste
Prepare as above. Put in a casserole with a tight-fitting lid. Pour on water, sprinkle with the sugar, cover and cook in the oven until tender.

2 Giving written directions

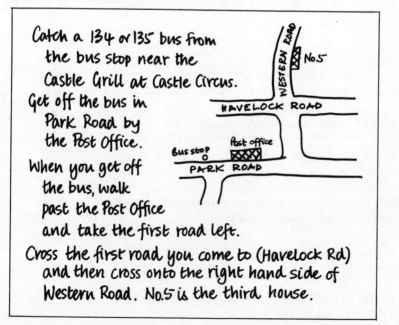

Catch a 134 or 135 bus from the bus stop near the Castle Grill at Castle Circus.
Get off the bus in Park Road by the Post Office.
When you get off the bus, walk past the Post Office and take the first road left.
Cross the first road you come to (Havelock Rd) and then cross onto the right hand side of Western Road. No.5 is the third house.

3 Technical instructions

A HACKER RADIO

Turn the radio on and increase volume by turning knob A to the right.

Select wavelength by choosing and depressing J (VHF/FM) K (MW) or L (LW).

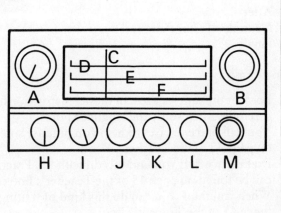

Select the right station by moving the red needle C to the left or right, with knob B.

Increase treble tone by turning knob H to the right. . .

LANGUAGE NOTES

Instructions (use dictionary form of verb):
    Prepare . . .
    Turn . . .
    Increase . . .
    Do not allow . . .

Strong instructions:
    You should allow . . .
    You shouldn't let . . .

Means (how to carry out instructions):
    . . . by turning it sharply to the left . . .
    . . . by means of . . .

Reasons:
    . . . in order to reduce the liquid . . .
    . . . to avoid the traffic . . .

Expected events or outcomes:
    It *should be* tender but whole.
    The meat is done when . . .

Sequencing:
First, second, third . . .
When . . .
Before -ing . . .
After . . .
Next, then, after that . . .
Finally . . .

WHAT TO DO

1 Look at the different sets of model instructions and read them carefully. Then study the language notes.
2 You will find exercises to help you practise some of this language on page 43 of the Teacher's Book.
3 Do Practice 1. If you find this difficult, do Practice 2. Extra practice can be found on page 45 of the Teacher's Book.
4 When you think you can do this kind of writing well, take a test (page 45 of the Teacher's Book).

Practice 1

Write out all three sets of instructions:

A *Recipe*
Perhaps you don't like English-made coffee very much. You know how to make coffee. Write out clear instructions for a friend or acquaintance.

B *Directions*
Write clear directions (with the help of a map if useful) from the place where you work to your home, so that a friend can find his way there.

C *Technical instructions*
Write instructions for the use of your cassette recorder (with the help of a labelled diagram if necessary or useful) so that someone else can operate it effectively.

Practice 2

Write out *three* of the four sets of instructions:

A *Procedures*
Write out a clear set of instructions for an acquaintance, about how he may join a public library in your country, and what obligations he has after joining.

B *Recipe*
Leave a recipe for one of your national cakes, puddings, or sweets for your hostess.

C *Technical instructions*
Explain how your alarm clock works, using a diagram if necessary.
or
Write brief instructions illustrating how your watch may be wound up / altered etc.

D *Directions*
With the help of a simple sketch map (if necessary) write a set of directions to a friend from the bus or railway station in your home town to your house or flat.

Section 4   Writing descriptions

Introduction

You may never have to write descriptions which are complete in themselves, but you may need to include descriptions in other pieces of writing, for example, in personal letters.

When you describe something, you are usually trying to give your reader an exact and detailed impression of something in your experience.

LANGUAGE NOTES: WORDS AND PHRASES

Since descriptions are concerned with detail, the larger and more precise your vocabulary, the better your descriptive writing will be. You should certainly be adequately equipped in the following categories:

a) place and position; direction
b) measurements: weight, size/volume, distance
c) shapes and patterns
d) colours and textures
e) materials and substances
f) technical vocabulary: faces and bodies, character, clothes, buildings, weather and so on
g) use and value

LANGUAGE NOTES: STRUCTURE

Most description concerns *universal qualities* or *constant and habitual processes*, and thus the present simple tense is in constant use. In descriptions of human scenes where there is activity or events occurring, then the other present tenses occur: present continuous and the present perfect.

● This section covers the following areas:
4.1   Describing people (physical descriptions, character etc.)
4.2   Describing places (towns, cities, villages)
4.3   Describing objects
4.4   Describing human scenes (commentary upon events happening *now*)
4.5   Describing landscape (natural scenes)
4.6   Describing habits and conditions (behaviour, customs, traditions)
4.7   Describing processes (how things work, operate)

Remember: The practices in this section are all based on real-life situations which require a written communication between two *English-speaking* people. Thus, when a task suggests that you write to a friend, acquaintance or organisation, it means an English-speaking person or organisation.

4.1 Describing people

Model

1 *Faces and bodies*
   Make sure you know all the words for facial features including *complexion*.
   How do we talk about *height* and *build*?
   Age: 'In his mid-forties'
   Remember early-
          mid-   forties
          late-
   Remember black-haired
           round-shouldered

Loose, wavy brown hair hung down to her waist at the back – she had a fringe over her forehead that almost hid her pale blue eyes. The nose – not her best feature – was long but not ugly. She had a regular set of white teeth and was full-lipped.

Her round face often looked rather sallow in complexion; she wasn't very tall or slim, and she walked with slightly-rounded shoulders.

When I knew her she must have been in her early thirties, about thirty-fivish even – and she even had one or two tell-tale wrinkles round the mouth.

2 *Clothes*
   He has a/an . . . *on.*
   He's *wearing* . . .
   He's *dressed in* . . .

I first met him at a small party and he was dressed in a rather ill-fitting suit with patches on the elbows; underneath there was an open-necked striped shirt. After that I don't think I ever saw him in a suit again. He mostly wore casual clothes – faded jeans, T-shirts, and open sandals.

3 *Facial and bodily expression*
He's frowning/scowling
He often has a grin on his face.
He looks ... + (adjective)
He looks as if he's ...
It looks/seems as though he ...

> People often thought of him as looking irritable but that was probably to do with his somewhat pink complexion and his bloodshot eyes. He flapped his hands quite a bit and rarely looked relaxed or calm. However, his face changed dramatically when he smiled, perhaps it was more of a boyish grin than a smile, and it altered one's view of him immediately.

4 *Character and habits*
She is always ...
She has the habit of ...

> She had the irritating habit of biting her nails but apart from that she was always welcoming and positive, once you knew her well. If you didn't, you might have thought her a bit stand-offish, but she wasn't really. Actually, she wasn't all that bright and often appeared intensely puzzled by life.

You may need to work on some language exercises first.

WHAT TO DO

1 Read each of the four model texts carefully, and look at the language notes which accompany each text. It is impossible to give all the language that can be used for personal descriptions in this book so you may need to do more reading and more language work before you start writing any descriptions yourself. (Ask your teacher about this.) However, there are some exercises in the Teacher's Book, page 48, to help you check your knowledge of the sort of language you need to write personal descriptions.

2 Write Practice 1. If you need more practice, do Practice 2; further
practice is found on page 51 of the Teacher's Book. These practices
ask you to concentrate on *physical* description.
3 Now do Practice 3, which asks you to write both physical and
character descriptions of people.
4 If you feel confident about your ability to write a reasonable
description of another person, take one of the two tests on page 52
of the Teacher's Book.

Practice 1

This practice concentrates on facial and bodily features, and clothing.
Look at the pictures and describe *both* as fully and interestingly as
possible:

Practice 2

This practice concentrates on facial and bodily features, and clothing.
Look at the picture and describe it as fully and interestingly as you can:

Practice 3

Try to do both A *and* B below. Concentrate on writing about the
following things:

Physical appearance – face
                               figure, body and gait
                               typical clothes
Character – facial and bodily expressions
                    habits and abilities
                    moods
                    general character

A Describe a teacher you've had at some time.

B Describe someone in your own family.

4.2 Describing places

Model

1 Read the following brief description of an English town:

> Oxford is an exceptionally old university town, on the River Thames, about 60 miles from London. Unlike modern university towns, where you usually find the university on the edge of the town, or on its own campus, Oxford's centre *is* the university; and all around the crossroads at the very heart of Oxford, Carfax, there are grey stone Colleges and other university buildings. In the centre you can also find interesting old pubs and paved passages. There are a lot of churches, and one or two really large and interesting buildings, such as the Ashmolean Museum, the 'round' library, the Bodleian and the Radcliffe Camera, with its domed roof. Like all English towns, there are parks, and one '*The* Parks', is the leafy home of university cricket in the summer months. As you leave the centre and go towards the outskirts of Oxford you can see industrial estates and a car factory in one direction; and in another, attractive (and expensive) suburbs. There is, in fact, quite a lot of industry in Oxford.

2 Now read this brief description of a park:

> As parks go, Mappin Park is large. Most of the flat ground is taken up by three football pitches and two rugby pitches. On one side of the park, however, there is a patch of trees through which a river winds. An attractive path runs beside the river, and there are flowerbeds with interesting shrubs and flowers. On the other side of the park from the river there are more sports facilities: three tennis courts and a bowling lawn. Near these, tucked into a corner, there is a children's playground with swings, seesaws and model vehicles. One of the pleasant features of the park is the fact that it is entirely surrounded by trees.

Writing descriptions

LANGUAGE NOTES

Location: *down by* the river/railway-station/*on* the river X
(very) *near* the bus-station
in the centre
on the outskirts / *in* the suburbs
in the (surrounding) countryside

Existence: there is/are
there has/have (always/never) been
it has been/stood there for/since
you can find/discover

Special features: ... of special interest is/are ...
one of the really/most interesting parts/places/
bits ...
the ... is famous/popular/etc. ...
you shouldn't miss (seeing/going to) ...

tourists | should / ought to | see/visit ...

WHAT TO DO

1 Read the model texts and the accompanying language notes.
2 Do Practice 1. If you or your teacher are not satisfied with your first
practice, do Practice 2. There are language exercises on page 53
and further practice will be found on page 56 of the Teacher's
Book.
3 If you think that you are able to write good descriptions of places
you can take a test. These are in the Teacher's Book on page 57.

Practice 1

Write *one* of the descriptions from A, and the description from B.

A Describe one of the places suggested below.
In your description, give the reader an idea of the size, location,
and type of city or town you're writing about. Mention interesting
or outstanding features; also mention how you feel about the
town, and what makes it an interesting (or depressing!) place for
you.

i) Your home town or village.

ii) A capital city you know well.

iii) Any British town, city or village that you know well, or have
lived in.

B Look at the plan of the garden below, and then write a description
   of it making sure that you give the reader a clear idea of what is in
   the garden, where things are in relation to each other, and what the
   garden is like generally.

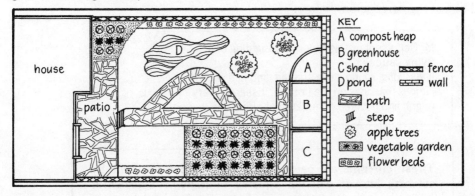

Practice 2

Write *one* of the descriptions in A, and the description in B:

A Describe one of the places suggested below:

   i)   London.

   ii) The town you're currently working in.

   iii) Any town you have lived in that isn't in Britain.

B Look at the plan of the riverside area shown below, and then write
   a description of it making sure that you give the reader a clear idea
   of what is in the area, where things are in relation to each other,
   and what the area is like generally.

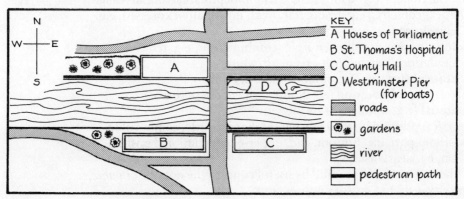

4.3 Describing objects

Model

Look at the descriptions below:

A

> Mr Denis sent us this report of a sighting of a
> **flying saucer:**
> It was long, round, cigar-shaped, and had several
> curious markings on the bottom. It seemed very
> bright, and hovered about 20 feet above the ground...

B

> **These curtains** are patchwork in design, and are made by
> stitching lots of different squares of material together in
> interesting colour combinations. Each curtain is about six feet
> long, and they hang from an old wooden rail, which has round
> wooden rings at intervals along it. The wood is dark, and the
> predominant colours in the curtains are white, light green, and
> russets, browns, and oranges.

C

> Vale Cottage is a roomy, 17th Century building, roughly an
> L-shape, built of limestone with walls about 22" thick.
> There are four downstairs rooms, and three up, including an
> attic room. The exterior has been painted off-white, and is
> rough in appearance...

LANGUAGE NOTES

When you describe objects you need language in the following categories:

measurements (e.g. width/height/length/depth/area/volume/weight)
shape (geometric, e.g. triangular, oval; informally-expressed, e.g.
   egg-shaped)
colour (pure, e.g. yellow, purple; combinations, e.g. reddy-brown;
   gradations, e.g. lightish-green, off-white)
texture of surfaces (e.g. smooth, ridged, bumpy)
pattern and decoration (e.g. floral, striped, criss-crossed)
material (e.g. wooden, brass, denim)
physical properties (e.g. transparent, hard, brittle, combustible)
position (part, e.g. bottom, end, upper-edge; relational position, e.g.
   on, by, near, inside)
Other categories that could be useful concern the notions of *value,
quality, use,* and *sensory impressions.*

WHAT TO DO

1 Read the model texts very carefully; as you can see from the language notes after the model, there is a lot of vocabulary associated with describing things; not all of this vocabulary can possibly be put into this book so you may have to do extra language work before you start on the writing tasks for this unit. Ask your teacher about this. You can do the exercises in the Teacher's Book, page 59.
2 Do Practice 1. If you or your teacher think you need to do more practice, do Practice 2; further practice is available in the Teacher's Book, page 62.
3 If you think that you can produce competent written descriptions of objects, you may take one of the two tests on page 62 of the Teacher's Book.

Practice 1

Describe all three objects suggested below:

A Describe the teapot and one other item in this picture.

B Describe this item of furniture. You need to hand your description to the police so that they can try to find it.

>>>→

65

C Describe in detail your shoes, your jacket, or your coat.

Practice 2

Describe all three objects suggested below.

A You accidentally left your hair-dryer, or your shaver, or your calculator, or your small radio with a friend in another town. Write her a description of it so that she can find it.

B You have just seen this unusual fish. Write a description of it so that an expert will be able to identify the fish.

C Write a description of this four-wheeled vehicle.

4.4 Describing human scenes

Model

Ruth is writing a letter to a friend of hers, describing the scene around her – she's staying with other friends in their ground-floor flat.

> The whole flat seems to be a hive of activity. In the kitchen the washing-machine's just stopped – it seems to have been going for ages – and Angela's taking the clothes out. I can only see soap-suds all over the top and down the sides. Margie is in the bedroom, trying to rouse Alan with a cup of tea which she has just made – he's been in bed since 9 last night – and now she's pulling the bed-clothes off him ... I think he's only pretending to be asleep. Outside there's a most peculiar couple – the man's just come out into the road holding a pullover he's been knitting and the woman has spent the whole morning under the car. She's now rather filthy and seems rather fed-up... I can hear her screaming at him. Ah! The door-bell has just rung – must go and see who it is!

LANGUAGE NOTES

Before you attempt to write your own descriptions think about the language used in Ruth's letter:

... has just stopped ...   (Completed actions)
... has just made ...

... is taking ...   (Activities happening at the
... is only pretending ...   present time)

... he's been knitting ...   (Activities that have
... it seems to have been going for ages ...   been going on for some
                                         time)

... seems, ... must, can ...

All these describe things going on *at* the moment or *up to* the moment.

WHAT TO DO

1 Read the model text and the language notes beneath it. Exercises on the sort of language you need for this unit can be found on page 64 of the Teacher's Book.
2 In Practice 1 you are asked to describe human scenes from a picture. If you need more practice do Practice 2.
3 Then do Practice 3 (and Practice 4, if you need to do more) which gives you more imaginative practice in describing human scenes.
4 You can do one of the tests on page 67 of the Teacher's Book if you are happy with your ability to describe human scenes adequately.

Practice 1

Imagine you are sitting outside the 'Plough Inn' writing to a friend. A description of the scene below forms part of your letter:

Practice 2

Imagine you are sitting outside 'The Bull' with the time to write a letter to a friend. A description of the scene below forms part of your letter:

Practice 3

Write *one* of the descriptions suggested below:

A   You are in prison for three months. It's November, and it's raining outside. You're rather depressed. In an attempt to conquer your depression write a description of your present 'scene' to a friend. Mention sounds and smells as well as what you can see.

   This *shouldn't* be a complete letter, but only part of one.

B   You're a tax-exile on a Caribbean island. At present you're on the beach, and quite content. In writing to a friend you happen to include a description of what the people around you are doing.

   This should only be *part* of a letter. There's no need to put address and date etc.

Practice 4

Write *one* of the descriptions suggested below:

A You live in an exceptionally noisy flat in an area you don't like –
   where, in your opinion, your neighbours have habits you really
   don't approve of.
      You are writing a letter of complaint to the local council.
   Include in your letter a description of the scene (sounds/sights/
   smells) around you, so that you convey your complaints in a
   practical and graphic fashion.

   Begin: ' . . . at this very moment two young hooligans . . . '

B It is a hot night in the centre of the city. You're in love. You can't
   sleep. Go onto the balcony of your hotel and write a letter to a
   close friend. Describe what you see going on around you, inside
   and outside the hotel.

   Don't write the whole letter – just the description part.

4.5 Describing landscape

Model

Unless you write travel brochures or similar literature, you may not need to describe landscape very often. However, you may want to include descriptions of landscape – if only a few details – in personal letters you write.

Look at this small landscape picture, and read the description.

My hotel room looks out across a main road which runs beside the river. To the left, about half a mile down the road there is a splendid-looking castle situated majestically on a small hill. The road bends right past this and crosses the river over a three-spanned stone bridge, entering a small village, whose church dominates the skyline. This village is set on a small hill, and beyond there are rolling hills right to the horizon, intersected by one or two tree-lined valleys...

LANGUAGE NOTES

Position:	right below me		100 yards away
	very near	about a	a quarter of a mile away
	a few yards away	in the middle distance	
	in the distance	on the left	
	on the horizon	to my right	
	on the skyline	on the right-hand side	

You may need to do some special vocabulary work in the following areas:

countryside vegetation and trees
weather
roads and paths
country buildings
rivers and water
hills and mountains
seascape and coast
feelings about landscape

Your teacher will be able to provide you with exercise work on these.

WHAT TO DO

1 Read the model text carefully. This text is only an example of landscape description, and does not contain all the language you need to write such descriptions. As you can see from the language notes, there is probably a lot of language you need to know before you start writing. Check this, if you think you need to, by doing the exercises in the Teacher's Book on page 70.
2 Do Practice 1. Your teacher will tell you whether you need to do Practice 2 or the further practice in the Teacher's Book on page 74.
3 When you are confident in your ability to write reasonable descriptions of landscape, you can take one of the tests available in the Teacher's Book on page 75.

Practice 1

Do *both* A and B:

A You are sitting on the river bank at Dittisham. Describe the scene before you:

DITTISHAM

B Now describe the scene you can see from your hotel or bedroom window:

Practice 2

Do *both* A and B:

A You're sitting on the river bank near Holne Bridge. Describe the scene before you:

HOLNE BRIDGE

B Now describe the scene you can see from your hotel or bedroom window:

4.6   Describing habits and conditions

Model

You may need to write about how someone lives; how someone
(yourself) works; leisure-habits or work-habits; the way something is
organised or works. These tasks all use the same sort of language.

1   Read this account of how the grandmother of the writer lives:

> ```
> My grandmother, a remarkable woman in some ways, lives alone in
> a North London flat, in a fiercely independent style.  From
> time to time someone ferries her over to north-east London to
> see my mother - her daughter - but usually it is my mother and
> the rest of the family who go to see her.  She does not seem to
> be lonely even though solitary.  She reads a great deal -
> mostly newspapers, and devours any information about Royalty -
> not that she professes royalism; she's just avidly curious
> about royal blood.  She reads in Swedish, her mother tongue,
> fairly frequently, and continues to keep up a lively
> correspondence with her younger sister in Stockholm.  She no
> longer sleeps very much, tending to rise at five in the morning
> to make tea.
>
>     She used to be something of a gastronome, but recently food
> has become almost irrelevant to her, even something of a
> nuisance.  I remember when she would eye up the salamis and
> exotic cheeses on the family table - now only birdseed keeps
> her going!
> ```

2   Now read a description (necessarily very brief) of some aspects of
Yugoslav life:

> The 'Yugoslavs' belong to five or six different cultures, speak four main languages, and several minor ones, and have very strong regional loyalties. In keeping with this pluralism, they claim to run a decentralised socialist economy in which local control is encouraged – well, to a certain extent. Decentralisation does not stop at geography; in theory it extends to each business and each enterprise: workers sit on committees in firms and universities and this is referred to as workers' self management! Many Yugoslavs have got into the habit of decrying this as being excessively cumbersome and bureaucratic; outside observers, however , remain – on the whole – impressed. One of the moral landmarks of Yugoslav economic life is that no man may earn three times more than *any* other man – a dictum not strictly observed but still rather impressive to any egalitarian.

LANGUAGE NOTES

Frequency: often/never; fairly often / quite frequently; every
weekend / twice a week
(Do you know where these expressions go in a sentence?)

Habit: (present habits)
He *likes* chocolate.
They *eat* at 6.

(past habits)
They *used to hang* sheep-stealers.
My father *would often bring* home gramophone records.
We *went every Saturday.*

(persistent and irritating habits)
They*'re always sending* me letters.
The tax people *keep reassessing* me.

Specific language problems are dealt with in the exercises which your
teacher will give you if you wish.

WHAT TO DO

1 Read these two model texts. Look at the brief language notes
which follow the texts. These will give you some help in writing
this sort of description, but this book cannot possibly predict what
other things you need to write in your practice descriptions.
  There are some exercises in the Teacher's Book, on page 78, if
you feel you need help before you start writing texts.
2 Do Practice 1. This gives practice in describing present habits and
conditions. If you need to do more practice because you or your
teacher think you need it, do Practice 2.
3 Practices 3 and 4 include a section on comparing present with past
habits and conditions. Do one or both practices.
4 When you think that you can do this sort of writing successfully, you
may like to take one of the tests on page 78 of the Teacher's Book.

Practice 1

Write *one* description, either A or B:

A A British man/woman is taking over your job for a year. Write an account
of the job – its responsibilities, the people you work for and with, its
difficulties etc. – to give your replacement a good idea of what it's like.

B A friend wants to know how people in your country tend to spend
their spare time – weekday evenings, weekends, national holidays,
actual holidays etc. Write an interesting account for him/her.

Practice 2

Write *one* piece, either A or B:

A The differences between your own life-style and that of your parents are interesting. Write an account of these differences between your life and your parents' life to a friend.

B You've been in England for a little while now. Write an account of English life – as you see it – to an English person in your country. You needn't write a complete letter, just write the description.
Ideas: food and drink? clothes? spare time? manners? children? schooling? political attitudes? emotions? sex? love? marriage?

Practice 3

Do *both* A and B:

A Describe how a normal week at your place of work is organised (times, breaks, variety, special activities) for a new English-speaking colleague due to arrive next month.

B Describe how people in your country meet members of the opposite sex, live with them, and marry them these days, *compared with* 100 years ago.

or

Describe in detail the differences between the way people travel now and the way they travelled before the 20th century.

Practice 4

Do *both* A and B:

A Describe what happens in your country during snow-storms, or heatwaves, or earthquakes.
In particular, describe people's reactions; procedures; official measures.

B People's attitudes to many aspects of life have changed in the last 50 years. Write a comparison between attitudes now and those 50 years ago in *one* of the following areas:
i)   clothes
ii) education
iii) sex
iv) women

4.7 Describing processes

Model

Although writing process descriptions is generally associated with the kinds of writing done by scientists, technicians and by other professional people, there are other occasions when you may need to describe a process.

The model text below gives a brief but precise description of what is involved in the marking of examination papers in foreign language examinations in Britain.

After the paper has been completed by the candidate, it is collected in by the invigilator, who bundles the papers together and places them, counted and labelled, in an envelope. They are then sent by recorded delivery to the chief examiner, who redistributes them for marking. The papers are marked initially by a single examiner, working with clear, predetermined marking guidelines. Problem papers are marked and returned to the chief examiner for remarking. In order to sample the marking the chief examiner selects a percentage of the papers from all examiners and marks them himself, or has them marked by a second marker. . . the process is rather time-consuming, and it is not customary in Britain to be informed of an examination result sooner than about two months from the time the examination was taken.

LANGUAGE NOTES

Notice that in this description both the *active* and the *passive* voices are used:
(passive)   . . . it is collected . . .
(active)   . . . the chief examiner selects a . . .
The passive is used frequently in process description in order to focus on and direct attention to the *object* of the process, and thus the process itself, and away from who or what is performing the process.
   It might be a good idea if you went through the model text and wrote down all the uses of the passive.

Means How something happens can be expressed by using some of
        the following:
        by means of
        through the use of   *or* | by | X
        with the help of | through | Y-ing

Purpose You sometimes need to say why something is done when
          describing a process:
                                  | to sample . . .
          10% are selected | in order to sample . . .
                                  | for sampling . . .

Process verbs The following verbs may be useful in writing process descriptions:
verbs describing process: occurs / happens / takes place / is carried out
verbs describing change: becomes / grows / turns / changes (into)

Sequencing Since processes occur in time, it is quite often necessary to say in what order things happen.

i)   before | X has been done / doing X
      until

ii) while
      as | Y is done / doing Y
      at the same time as

iii) when
      after   Z is done   on doing Z
      once   after doing Z
      as soon as   having done Z

You can just use a phrase followed by a comma:

before this, / previously,
during this time / process, / meanwhile,
after this, / later,

Modality Some things depend on restrictions or circumstances:
... at this point the water *must be added*.
... then sugar *can be stirred* in.
If you want a quick reply, the letter *should be taken* to the central post office and registered.

WHAT TO DO

1 Read the model text and the language notes very carefully. If you feel you would like to practise some of this language before you start writing process descriptions, ask your teacher for the exercises on page 80 of the Teacher's Book.
2 Do Practice 1. If you or your teacher are not satisfied with your first practice, do Practice 2. Extra practice is available on page 82 of the Teacher's Book.
3 When you think that you can write process descriptions, you can take Test 1 or 2. These are on page 82 of the Teacher's Book.

N.B. Please note that this unit does not concern the writing of instructions for processes. If you want to learn to write process instructions, turn to Unit 3.3.

Practice 1

Do *both* A and B.

A Describe precisely *how* people are admitted to hospital in your country – just in case any of your acquaintances should ever need to know.
   Mention: calling ambulance / private car
   form-filling
   contacting relatives
   contacting usual doctor

B Describe in detail the preparations made in your town/city/village for a festival, special holiday or carnival.

Practice 2

Do *both* A and B:

A Describe precisely *how* passports or residence permits are obtained in your country. A friend may need the latter one day.
   Mention: personal actions
   bureaucratic processes

B Describe, in detail, what happens to young recruits in the army in your country and how they are trained.

Section 5   Reporting experiences

Introduction

The units in this section belong to two separate parts:
Reporting actions and events   (Units 5.1, 5.2, 5.3)
Reporting speech   (Unit 5.4)

Reporting actions and events

5.1 Reporting incidents and events
5.2 Writing biographical information
5.3 Narrating

These units involve using similar writing skills and use of language. The differences between the three units are that Unit 5.1 concerns the reporting of isolated events (the kind of writing we do in most letters of an anecdotal sort); Unit 5.2 reports sequences of isolated *or* connected events in people's lives; Unit 5.3 involves extended and descriptive reporting of the past.

   For these three units you ought to be able to use the past tenses in English clearly and accurately. This involves the ability to:

report
- past actions (completed)
- incomplete or interrupted actions in the past,
- past habits, conditions, and states
- actions (complete or incomplete), habits, states and conditions preceding an event in the past

sequence and order events in the past
describe things in the past (as appropriate)

Reporting speech

5.4 Reporting speech

Before you attempt this unit, check that you know how English people do this – the 'rules' are probably different from the way you report speech in your own language. You will find an exercise section on page 96 of the Teacher's Book to help you.
You should also have a reasonable range of speech words (e.g. mention, suggest, deny etc.).

   You may never need to report long pieces of speech in a written form – but you are always likely to want to report small bits of speech, in letters, in narrative and in reports. This unit could then prove very useful, especially as we report *thought* in the same ways as speech.

There is a direct application of this unit in 7.3, Summary reports, Practice 3 (summarising speeches).

Remember: The practices in this section are all based on real-life situations which require a written communication between two *English-speaking* people. Thus, when a task suggests that you write to a friend, acquaintance or organisation, it means an English-speaking person or organisation.

5.1 Reporting incidents and events

Model

A narrative is a story. Inside a narrative you often have to write about single *incidents* or simple *events*. Naturally the past tenses are used, as shown below:

LANGUAGE NOTES

The fire brigade *arrived* (1) very soon after the fire *had started* (2) although it *had* probably *been smouldering* (3) for some hours and *would have broken* out sooner (4) if the place hadn't been so damp; anyway, it *wasn't burning* (5) very furiously when the fire engine turned up.	Past action complete (1) Action completed before a time in the past (2) Something happens before and up to a time in the past (3) A hypothesis about the past (4) A past action incomplete or interrupted (5)

Linking words are also used in this kind of writing, particularly the following sorts:

time links e.g. 'They arrived soon *after* the fire had started.'
causal links e.g. 'The fire wasn't very serious *as/because* the place was damp.'
contrast links e.g. '*Although* the fire had probably been smouldering for hours, it still wasn't burning very furiously when the fire engines arrived.'

82

1 Read the account of an incident below:

> Frank was definitely not expecting any visitors to his room that afternoon and indeed he had just begun to snooze in the mild afternoon sunshine when someone tapped lightly on the door. Long before Frank could respond to the knock, the handle turned and two children sidled in. While the first, a slightly gipsy-looking child wandered over to the window, the other leaned over Frank's desk and placed a large box on the top. There was a short silence, and then both children edged towards the door. They said nothing, not a word, and Frank too failed to find his voice; they had gone before he could protest. He looked uneasily at the box.

2 Now read this less studied, more conversational account of a small misfortune at work – a girl is writing to a friend:

> Well – I'd only just got to my desk with these two steaming cups of coffee when a hand suddenly tapped me on the back – I jumped a mile, right out of my skin, the cups flew out of my hand, and one of them landed on the boss's knee ... as the hot coffee went through the material he let out a yell – he was phoning at the time! – so you can imagine that I wasn't his blue-eyed favourite for the rest of the morning!

WHAT TO DO

1 Read both the more formal and the conversational model texts of the reporting of incidents and events. Look at the accompanying language notes. If you want to practise that sort of language before you start writing texts, ask your teacher for the exercises which are on page 84 of the Teacher's Book.
2 Do both parts of Practice 1: A is based on a picture, and B on your own experiences or imagination. If you need to do more practice, do Practice 2; further practice may be found on page 86 of the Teacher's Book.
3 If you find that you can do this sort of writing quite well, you can take one of the two tests for this unit on page 87 of the Teacher's Book.

Practice 1

Do both A and B:

A Below you can see a picture of a demonstration. Report this event, using the ideas beneath the picture to help you.

The report should be in the past.

Ideas: 21 June 1983   historic house
           redevelopment   protest
           peaceful   speeches
           press/photographers   owners' anger
           profitable to sell   poor condition

B Write a short account of an incident in public when

  i)   someone tried to snatch your bag.   *or*

  ii)   you saw a man trying to steal someone's wallet.   *or*

  iii) you saw a woman accusing a person of short-changing her.

Practice 2

Do both A and B:

A Below you can see a picture of an incident that happened on a
  mountain somewhere. Report the incident, using the ideas beneath
  the picture to help you.

Ideas:	23 February 1983	broken leg
	very long wait	life in danger
	rescue attempts	icy winds
	other climbers	charge of 'recklessness'

B Write an account of an incident you saw once, when a woman at a
  bus stop fainted. Set the scene; say what happened; describe the
  consequences and reactions; conclude.

5.2 Writing biographical information

Model

You may at some time need or want to write a report on someone's life, or even a report on your own life!

Read the following report (taken from a Bradford newspaper) on the life of a Mr Anthony Sinclair:

Anthony George Sinclair was born on December 14, 1942. He was the first child of a family of three boys and two girls.

After attending Potternewton Infants and Junior schools he went to Chapeltown Secondary Modern School.

He left there with no qualifications and went to work as a commis waiter at the Queens Hotel in Leeds. It was the first of a long series of jobs.

Until he was 18 he worked as a warehouseman at several firms and then spent two years as a bus conductor.

He signed on in the Army but stayed only ten weeks before he bought himself out for £25.

After working as a warehouseman, he joined the Leeds Corporation Parks Department where for six years he was a gardener.

It was during this period that Sinclair decided to better himself and after passing six GCEs he was about to start a teacher training course at Bradford. During the holidays he worked as a waiter and cleaner at a Pontins holiday camp.

Sinclair's ambition, with his work as a team manager with the Pudsey Junior football team, was to become a physical education teacher.

LANGUAGE NOTES

When people *do* things, English uses the active:
He/she went ...
       left ...
      worked as ...
      spent a lot of time ...

When things *happen* to people, the passive is used:
He/she was born and brought up in ...
      was educated at ...
      was given a job ... dismissed ...
      was injured in a car crash ...

Time sequences
– after and before:
 After this, he went ...
 After taking his exams, he went ...

 Before this, he had worked in ...
 Before moving south, he bought ...
 Until then, he lived/she had lived ...
– same time:
 During this period, he became ill ...
 While working at ..., he got interested ...
 While he was working at ...
 It was then that he became involved with ...

WHAT TO DO

1 Read the model. Look at the language notes.
2 Do both parts of Practice 1. If you or your teacher are not satisfied
 with it, do Practice 2. Further practice will be found on page 90 of
 the Teacher's Book.
3 When you are happy with your writing of this unit you may take a
 test (page 91 of the Teacher's Book).

Practice 1

Write A and *one* from B:

A Write an imaginary life-story from the following details:

 Elizabeth Reynolds – b. 1935 – d. 1976 (suicide) – childhood:
 Yorkshire mining village – wrote first poems – hated school – first
 job, village shop for 7 years – to London 1957 – published poems
 and first novel – became depressed – 1960 first suicide attempt –
 married and quickly divorced (1965) – America – lost earlier
 popularity – had 'love-child' 1971 – moved to Cornwall 1973 ...

B Write a short obituary notice for a famous writer, musician,
 painter, or politician from your country – imagine he/she suddenly
 died last week.

 or

 Write a brief biographical account of any famous historical figure.

Practice 2

Do both A and B:

A Write an imaginary life-story out of the following biographical
   notes:

1899	born in Stockholm, Sweden
1905–1917	schooling – fluent in German, English, French, Swedish
1918 and after	translators' school and then Government translator
1922	to Germany – freelance
1924 and after	met/married British businessman – settled London
1925 and after	had first of 4 children
1928	eldest child died
1930	series of translations of Swedish, Danish, Norwegian poets into English
1937	husband died
1940	volunteer nurse in war
1945	returned to Sweden
1946	remarried to poet and dramatist
1951	car accident – died

B Write a short biographical sketch of any character in a novel or a
   play that you know well enough. If this is difficult, write a
   biographical sketch of a character in a film.

5.3 Narrating

Model

A narrative is usually thought of as a piece of writing that tells a complete 'story'. But this kind of writing includes a number of different types.

1 First of all there is factual writing which includes historical and biographical accounts, and real life reports like the example below.

The day a lonely killer became their friend

AS Andre Retat and his wife Raymonde arrived at the gates of the Muret maximum security jail in Toulouse, they almost turned back.

They were there to visit a killer and did not relish the idea. But they were determined to keep the promise they had made to the local priest who was a prison visitor.

For the wealthy butcher and his wife, a devoutly religious couple anxious to be involved in community work, had been touched when Father Gendreau had told them of the convict they had come to see.

"He was jailed at the age of 18," the priest had said. "Now he is totally alone. For he is an orphan and in the four years he has been in jail he has not had one visitor. He is badly in need of help. Will YOU help?"

from
DAVID PASKOV
Paris

That was how the Retats found themselves face to face with Alain Cimmino who was serving a 15-year sentence for killing his lover.

The visit went well. Cimmino was shy, well-mannered and did not moan about his luck nor ask for food, cigarettes or even books. The Retats became regular visitors and Cimmino became a model prisoner.

When, on one occasion, he blurted out to the Retats: "You cannot imagine how much your visits mean to me," Andre replied: "Don't worry. You are no longer on your own. We won't let you down."

And the Retats kept their word. With their guarantee for his good conduct, Cimmino was released five years early and the Retats took him into their own home and gave him a job at Andre's butcher's shop.

Before long Cimmino realised that they were not the happy couple they appeared to be. Although neither had sought solace in the company of anybody else, they slept in different bedrooms and had once talked about separating.

When, one day, 29-year-old Cimmino gently asked Raymonde, 45, if she was truly happy, she confided : " No, there are times when I feel so alone."

That was when the once lonely Cimmino became Raymonde's lover. The affair continued for several months before 48-year-old Andre became suspicious and confronted the man he had befriended.

There was a fierce argument which ended when Cimmino shot Andre dead. Last week Cimmino began a new jail sentence . . . this time for life. Once again he looks like being the loneliest convict in the prison. For Raymonde, who had admitted their affair in court, refuses to visit him.

And Father Gendreau, the priest who persuaded the Retats to give Cimmino another chance, cannot be found.

Said Cimmino's lawyer, Georges Catala : " We tried to find him to be a witness at Cimmino's trial. But he had moved on four or five years previously and could not be traced."

2 Secondly, there is fictional writing: novels, short and long stories, jokes and fictional anecdotes.

The example below is the first two paragraphs of a short story.

Mary stared through the trees into the distance as it dissolved slowly before her eyes in the creeping darkness. The park lights came on suddenly and made her start. She did not know how long she had been sitting there or what she had been thinking about. She only knew that it was dark, wet and cold and she had nowhere to go. She could not move from the bench. Her body felt heavy and her legs felt as if they would not carry her. She tried hard to remember how she had come to be there, but could not. Footsteps echoed down the empty path towards her, and for the first time in her life, she was afraid.

She had felt so strong that morning, so determined. Why shouldn't she try to get a place of her own? All she was to Janice and Doug was an unpaid housekeeper, babysitter and cook. And she paid them twenty pounds a week for the privilege! Even now she bristled with indignation at the thought of it.

LANGUAGE NOTES

It is impossible to predict all the language you will need to write a complete narrative; you will always need to *describe* things in narrative and these descriptions will be unique to the narrative you are writing.

However, narrative usually involves expressing what happens in time, so the following areas of language are very important:

a) tense and time
  'they almost *turned* back' (completed past action)
  'he *was serving* a jail sentence' (incomplete past action)
  'determined to keep the promise they *had made*' (completed action before a time in the past)
  'she *had been crying* when he first saw her' (unfinished action before a time in the past)

b) sequencing links
   first / at first / right from the start / at the beginning
   before long / previously
   then / after that / next
   It was then that ...
   The next thing was that ... / to ...
   That was when ...
   Finally / In the end / Eventually

c) time–relation links
   when / once / as soon as / immediately
   after / before
   while / as

d) structural links
   '*Left* alone, she panicked.'
   '*Waving* goodbye to his home town, Philip felt sick at heart.'

e) time reference
   on (a day) in (a year/week/month) at (weekend/Festival)
   at (clock time) during (year/month)
   about/around (clock time)
   last week / one day / on one occasion

WHAT TO DO

1 To practise *fictional* writing, do Practice 1. If you need to do more
  than one practice because your first attempt is not good enough, do
  Practice 2; there is further practice in the Teacher's Book, page 92.
2 To practise *factual* narrative, do Practice 3. If you need to do more
  practice, do Practice 4, or Extra Practice 2, in the Teacher's Book,
  page 93.
3 As a final practice, you might like to write a continuation of the
  story which begins in the model. When you have written your
  story, read the original version in the Teacher's Book, page 163.
4 Tests 1 and 2, which you must write on your own, will be found in
  the Teacher's Book, on page 94.

Practice 1

Write *both* A and B:

A A friend of yours has asked you to write out a fairy tale or folk tale
   that you know – perhaps one that comes from your country – to
   read to young children.
   Write out such a story in simple, plain English. Try not to write
   much more than 100 words unless you really have to.

B There are eight pictures below which tell a story from human life.
There are also one or two words written in some of the boxes.
Write out this story as well as you can.
  You may start, if you like, with this idea:

'The Gregory's – Paula and Alan – were delighted when a young
couple moved into the house next door . . .'

Practice 2

Write *both* A and B:

A In a letter to a friend, you want to tell him/her about a film you went to – a film with a powerful story.

   Using no more than 150 words write out the story of the film as clearly as possible.

B There are seven pictures below which tell a story from human life. There are also one or two words written in some of the frames. Write out this story as clearly as you can.

   You may start, if you like, with this idea:

'Erika had always been an exceptionally independent person, who dressed and acted in a somewhat individualistic way. On the night of 18 February, she went to a friend's party . . . '

Practice 3

This practice concerns the narrative of real life: A gives you practice
in narrating historical episodes; B asks you to narrate something
which is personal.

A *Cuba Missile Crisis*
   In the autumn of 1962, the Americans and the Russians faced each
   other in a very serious international incident after the Americans had
   discovered that the Russians were building nuclear missile sites on
   the island of Cuba.

   Look at the series of events (written in note form below) which
   lead up to this crisis and then use the notes and the map to write a
   narrative account of this piece of recent history.

Jan. 1959	Castro takes power in Cuba.
	Cuba turns communist.
1962	Americans worried about world communism.
July 2	Raul Castro (Cuba War Minister) – Moscow visit.
July and Aug.	Russian ships, Russian technicians to Cuba (5,000 by end of August).
Sept.	Reports: nuclear missiles in Cuba?
Oct.	Rumours of six missile sites being built in Cuba.
Oct. 14	American planes photograph Cuba.
Oct. 15	Photo analysis. Nuclear missile sites.
Oct. 16	President Kennedy told. Special meeting to discuss plans.
Oct. 17	New photos. Perhaps 32 sites ready in ten days.
Oct. 19	American Govt. decide to blockade Cuba.
Oct. 21	43 other governments told.
Oct. 22	Kennedy speaks to Americans on TV. No reaction from Russians.
Oct. 24	Blockade of Cuba begins. Russian ships still sailing to Cuba. Missile sites still being built in Cuba.

Oct. 25	Russian ships stop, some turn round.
Oct. 27	Russians demand end to American bases in Turkey. America 'no'.
Oct. 28	Russians promise removal of nuclear missiles from Cuba. Crisis ends.

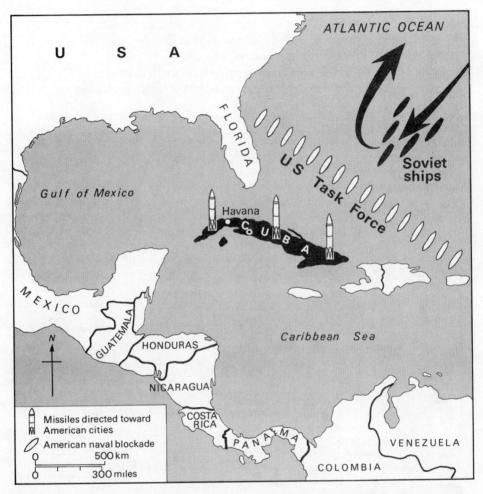

B Every family has fascinating bits of family history. Think about your family (parents, grandparents, uncles, aunts, brothers, sisters) and pick out an interesting piece of family history, which you want to write about to a friend. Now write this out as clearly as possible.

Practice 4

This practice (like Practice 3) asks you to narrate a story from real life: A will offer you practice at narrating something from recent history; B asks you to narrate something related to your country.

A *Bay of Pigs Incident*

In April, 1961, a group of exiled Cubans tried to invade Cuba and depose the new President, Fidel Castro.

Look at the series of events leading up to this, written in note form below and use them and the map to write a narrative account of this recent piece of history.

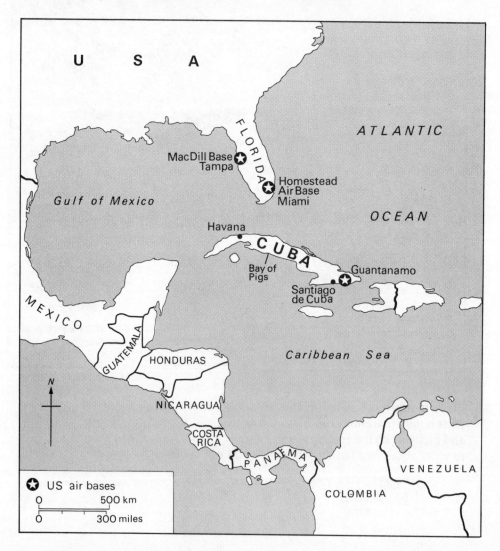

Jan. 1959	Castro takes power in Cuba.
	Visits America as 'liberal democrat'.
1959	Cuba becomes communist.
	Cuban liberals into exile (with help of C.I.A.).
	C.I.A. create counter-revolutionary group 'La Brigada' – exiled Cubans (professionals: lawyers, doctors, teachers etc.) training in Guatemala.
Nov. 1960	Kennedy wins election.
	Kennedy informed of 'La Brigada'.
Feb. 1961	C.I.A. pressure on Kennedy to send 'La Brigada' to attack Cuba. Hesitation.
April 10	'La Brigada' to Nicaragua.
April 13	Onto boats.
April 15	Some of Castro's airforce destroyed in Cuba.
April 16	Castro arrests all likely counter-revolutionaries.
April 17	'La Brigada' attack Cuba in Bay of Pigs. Seen and reported to Castro.
April 18	Cuban army surround invasion force.
	American rescue attempt fails.
April 20	All over – rebels arrested.
Rest of 1961	Kennedy criticised in and out of America.

B School life is usually rich in stories. Think about the schools you went to and pick out an interesting episode that you were part of or knew about from your school life. Now write it down as if it were part of a letter to a friend. Try to be clear and interesting.

5.4 Reporting speech

Model

A is a transcript of an interview broadcast by the BBC with the actor,
Sir John Gielgud, and B is a report of that interview. Read them both
and compare them.

A Interview	B Report of Interview
I: Was it easy for you when you were young?	When Sir John was asked (3) if it had been (1) easy for him (2) as a young man, he emphatically denied (3) that it had been easy (1) or that it was now (1).
G: No – it wasn't – indeed not – it still isn't.	
Acting – true acting – never really gets any easier because the demands made of an actor will always be the same.	He explained (3) that true acting never really got (1) any easier and that this was (1) because the demands made of an actor would (1) always be the same.
I: The same? What do you mean by that?	When asked what he meant by this (2), he said that whether he was (1) there (2) or at Pinewood or on stage one had to (1) beware of the banal and the tawdry.
G: Well...whether I'm here, or at Pinewood, or on stage, one must beware of the banal and the tawdry.	

LANGUAGE NOTES

When you report speech, even small snatches of speech, you must
remember three things: (these are marked 1, 2, 3 in passage B).

1 After a past tense speech verb (told/asked/said) all tenses move
  back in time. Look at examples of (1) above. When questions are
  reported there is both shifted tense and also changed word order.
2 When speech is reported some reference words of time and
  location change. Look at examples of (2) above.
3 There are many 'speech' words in English, and you will find some
  of them illustrated above (3).

WHAT TO DO

1 Read the short model text for this unit. This text shows both the kind of text you will need to write (on the right) and the origin of the text (on the left). Study this, and also the language notes beneath the text.

   The 'rules' for reporting speech are quite precise in English, and may be very different from those of your own language. You might find it helpful to complete the exercises for this unit, in the Teacher's Book on page 96.
2 Do Practice 1. If you need more practice, do Practice 2. More practice can be found on page 98 of the Teacher's Book.
3 Once you feel confident of your ability to report speech and make it part of a full text, you may want to take one of the tests for this unit. These are on page 99 of the Teacher's Book.

Practice 1

Write *both* A and B:

A Johnny, a 13-year-old boy, is in a magistrates' court for breaking into the house of a neighbour. Report the conversation between the magistrate and the boy.

M: Stand up, Johnny, I want to talk to you.
    Now ... how much money did you have on you when you went into Mrs Aylot's house.
J: Five pounds, sir.
M: If you had that much, what made you want to steal more?
J: Don't know, sir. Suppose it was a big thing to do.
M: Is that what your friends do?
J: Mmm ... yes, sometimes, some of them. They say rich people don't need all their money.
M: Do you agree with that?
J: Don't know.

B On the next page you'll find an advertisement, published in a British magazine.
What does the advert *warn*?
What does it *claim*?
What does it *insinuate*?
What does it *suggest/advise*?
At the end, what does it *add*?

Joy-Rides
JUNIOR TRAVEL-SICKNESS TABLETS

PREVENT · TRAVEL · SICKNESS

MAKE JOY-RIDES PART OF YOUR JOURNEY.

If your children are travelling by car, boat, plane or train, make sure travel-sickness doesn't spoil their journey.

Take along a packet of Joy-Rides.

Joy-Rides are raspberry-flavoured and chewable. They're not sweets; they're the first travel-sickness tablets made specially for children.

Each tablet is a precisely measured child's dose, although two tablets work very effectively even on an adult.

And Joy-Rides can quickly clear up travel-sickness even after it's come on.

So when you're taking along the children, take along the Joy-Rides.

You'll all feel better for it.

There's a free book you can get too, to make your journeys even happier. It's 'I Spy On A Car Journey,' and you'll find details at your chemists.

STAFFORD-MILLER

Joy-Rides are now available in the Republic of Ireland.

Practice 2

Write both A and B:

A This is a conversation between an old woman and a young man in the foyer of a hotel. Begin your piece of writing with the words, 'I overheard a man talking to an old woman ... he came in and ....'

Man: Excuse me. Are you sure the nine-sixteen is still only for Paris?

W: I'm afraid so, sir. Next year they're going to start an air-service three times a week, but in the meanwhile ... Here's your key.

Man: I'm not going up thanks. Could you call Paris. The number's 89–26.

W: Certainly, sir ... 89–26 ... it'll be through in five minutes ... yes. Ah ... there's also a telegram for you!

Man: Yes, I was quite expecting it. Keep it here for me for the moment. (Pause) Has this place changed much in the last few years ... I mean, who owns it now?

W: Don't really know ... the Esters?

Man: No – not the Esters. You don't know then?

W: I'm afraid not.

B The following is a speech by Mrs Margaret Thatcher, when Conservative Leader. Report what she said using the following words:
promised asserted claimed warned emphasised denied

'I intend to put national interest above my party's. For the Conservative Party, politics has always been about more than gaining power. It has been about serving the nation. And now we need to know it. Britain is at the end of the road. As we all know, Mr Heath first said this, and he's a man whose sincerity could not be doubted. Under Labour the land of hope and glory has become the land of beg and borrow. Do we want such policies? We don't!'

Section 6 Writing to companies and officials

Introduction

This section concerns the writing of forms or letters to companies or officials in institutions and Government offices as an *individual*.

N.B. Please note that this section is not about the writing of letters by managers or secretaries *from* companies and institutions. That uses specialist English and often uses fixed phrases and formulas that are not necessary for an individual writer to use.

Official letter-writing, like personal letter-writing, is not difficult in English, if your purpose is simple. Formal letter-writing doesn't need to use elaborate or flowery language of any sort; the writing should just be *clear*.

Below there is an example of how people nearly always set out their letters in English to commercial companies and officials. Look at it, and carefully study the notes that go with it. You can use this outline model for Units 6.2 to 6.7.

```
                                        116, Faversham Road,
                                  (A)   Marden,
                                        Kent,
     (C) Your ref:  TG/782              KT9 4TY

     (D) The Personnel Manager,   (B)   8th June, 1983
         The 'Y' Hotel,
     (E) Tottenham Court Road,
         London WC1 2LZ

     (F) Dear Mr/Mrs Vaughan/Sir/Madam/Sirs/Sir or Madam,

               (G) I recently saw a(n)....
              LETTER

                    (H) Yours sincerely,
                        Yours faithfully,

                    (I) Alan Rowley .

                    (J) Alan Rowley
```

NOTES

(A) *Your* personal address goes in the *top right-hand corner*. Do *not* put your address at the bottom of the letter. Do *not* put your name above or near your address, even if this is what you do in your own language! Remember always to use the postcode! (e.g. KT9 4TY)

(B) The date always goes under your address, and can be written in a number of acceptable ways: 8th June, 1983; 8/6/83; 8.6.83; June 8, 1983. Be careful – Americans write this last date in numbers as 6/8/83, the British *always* put the day first, followed by the month, 8/6/83.

(C) If the company or the official has written to you before, there may be a reference number on the previous letter. Quote this back to the writer, on the left-hand side as shown.

(D) Try to write down either the *name* or the *position* of the person you are writing to, or both if you know them.

(E) Write down the name of the company or institution that you're writing to, and then the official address – the address needn't be the full postal address. The name and address of the company can also be written beneath your signature at the bottom of the letter.

(F) The normal ways of naming the person you are writing to are as follows:
   i) if you know the name   Dear + Mr/Mrs/Ms/Miss + Surname
      of the person
   ii) if you don't know   Dear + Sir/Madam / Sir or Madam / Sirs
       the name of the person   N.B. *Dear Sir* is the normal form here

(G) The first line of the letter usually starts below the end of the name of the person you are writing to, but you can start your letter on the left-hand side, underneath the name.

(H) When you know the name of the person you are writing to, use the form *yours sincerely*. If you don't know the name of the person you are writing to, it is usual to use the form *yours faithfully*.

(I) You should write your signature here.

(J) Below your signature you should *print* your name, so that the person who reads your letter is in no doubt about who you are!

● This section covers the following areas:

6.1 Filling in forms. This is not letter-writing but the sending of information to companies and institutions on forms. There are practices for simple forms, forms involving money, and job and educational applications.

6.2 Writing letters *requesting* goods, services, or information.

6.3 Writing *application* letters for education, jobs etc., including the writing of curriculum vitae.

6.4 Writing letters which *give information*.

6.5 Writing letters which *give instructions*.

6.6 Writing letters which *complain* about something you dislike or object to.

6.7 Writing letters of *apology*.

Each unit will make suggestions about useful and appropriate language for such letters in the *Language notes*.

Remember: The practices in this section are all based on real-life situations which require a written communication between two *English-speaking* people. Thus, when a task suggests that you write to a friend, acquaintance or organisation, it means an English-speaking person or organisation.

6.1 Form-filling

Model

There is little point in giving *one* model for form-filling since forms are used for a very great variety of purposes. Each form is, to some extent, unique.

However, some *terms* are common to many forms and these items are written out below.

COMMON TERMS ON FORMS

Forenames/first name/ Christian name(s)	(e.g. John)
Surname/family name	(e.g. Smith)
Signature	(how you usually write your name)
Full name	(Christian name and surname)
Initials	(first letters of all names e.g. D.N.R. or first letters of Christian names e.g. D.N.)

Age	
Sex	
Marital Status:	
Married	
Single	(not married yet)
Divorced	
Separated	(living legally apart from wife/husband)
Widowed	(husband/wife has died)

Date of birth	
Date of purchase	(the date you bought something)
Date	(the date when you fill in the form)

Address:	
Permanent	(your normal address in your own country)
Temporary	(where you are living – for a while – now)
Home	(your or your parents' normal address)
Work	(the address of where you work)
… in X months' time	(future address)

Tel. No.	(telephone number)
Passport No.	
Bank Acc. No.	(bank account number)
Your ref:	(your reference number in business letters)
Our ref:	(the reference number of the company you're writing to)

You'll often see the following two expressions:

| BLOCK CAPITALS | (write in big/capital letters) |
| PLEASE PRINT | (do not use script writing) |

In this unit there is no test. The following practices are available.

Practice 1 Simple forms
Practice 2 Money: insurance and assurance
Practice 3 Education application form
Practice 4 Job application form

Always read forms carefully, *before* you fill them in!

WHAT TO DO

1 There is no model text for this unit. Filling in forms does not involve you in writing a text but in completing one, with your own personal information.

   Read carefully through the list of common terms found on forms. Use a dictionary, or ask your teacher, to make sure you understand all of them.

2 Do the practices you find most useful, but you should do Practice 1.
   Further practice of simple forms will be found on page 103 of the Teacher's Book.
   Further practice of forms involving money will be found on page 106 of the Teacher's Book.
   Further practice of forms for educational or training applications will be found on page 110 of the Teacher's Book.
   Further practice of forms for job applications will be found on page 111 of the Teacher's Book.
   N.B. Only fill in these forms if this book is yours. If this is not your book, copy out the headings into your notebook and then fill them in.

3 There are no tests for this unit.

Practice 1   Simple forms (sending for goods and information)

Fill in all the forms below:

A

FREE INFORMATION PACK

We'd like to tell you much more about how we are helping by sending you a copy of our new Information Pack 'Oxfam and You'. This contains a special message from James Cameron and details of how we put every pound to the best possible use.

Name_____

Address_____

_____

_____

Postcode_____

Room, TR03 Oxfam, 274 Banbury Road, Oxford OX2 7DZ.

B

Please send me, without obligation; (please tick)

FREE FUND RAISING GUIDE ☐   FREE 116 PAGE CHRISTMAS CATALOGUE ☐

Details of Approval Parcel and how to obtain FREE a super Travel Bag or a Coffee System ☐

Name _____   **FR6H**

Fund Raising Cause _____

Address _____

_____ Postcode _____

We reserve the right to refuse any application and to apply credit restrictions at our discretion.

♛ **Webb Ivory Limited, Little Cornbow, Halesowen, West Midlands B63 3AG**

C

If you wear wide-fit shoes

J. D. Williams will solve your problems and save you the trouble and expense of shopping and searching! We stock a large selection of Standard 'C' to Ultra Wide 'EEE' up to size 9 in Ladies' Footwear.

The range features many famous brands shown in colour including Brevitt, Diana, Draper, Pirelli, Portland, Duraflex, K Shoes, Lotus and Trustyle. Try any shoes you choose, at home, in comfort and see how wide-fitting shoes can look smart yet feel comfy.

In addition to your statutory rights you are guaranteed full refund of any money sent if you are not completely satisfied.

SEND NOW FOR **FREE** CATALOGUE

10 MONTHS TO PAY

APR **30·6%** **VARIABLE**

EASY CREDIT TERMS AVAILABLE TO ALL CUSTOMERS
NO INQUISITIVE FORMS TO FILL IN
**J.D. Williams & Co Ltd (Dept. 37/109) PO Box 285
The Dale St. Warehouses. Manchester. M60 6ES**

109   Please send my personal copy of the latest J. D. Catalogue *FREE!* I understand there will be no obligation or callers

Mrs/Miss _____
Block Capitals Please
Address _____

Town _____

County _____   Postcode _____

We reserve the right to refuse application.   Credit over 18 only.

D

John Gooders
WHERE TO WATCH BIRDS

The Classic Guide to Bird-Watching in Britain

SPECIAL OFFER FROM RSPB

£1.50 OR FREE

When you join the RSPB from this advertisement

Wherever you go there's a wealth of bird life to watch. 'Where to Watch Birds' **is a 343 page guide to the best sites** – how to get there and what to expect at what time of year. With maps and map references.

John Gooders scored an immediate success when this book was first published.

This essential book can be yours FREE when you become a member of the Royal Society for the Protection of Birds.

Your annual subscription will help us to buy more land where birds can live in safety, to fight even harder against the many threats faced by birds today.

Send your subscription now and claim your Free copy of 'Where to Watch Birds'. FREEPOST RSPB, The Lodge, Sandy, Bedfordshire SG19 2DL.

FREEPOST RSPB, The Lodge, Sandy, Bedfordshire SG19 2DL (Please allow 21 days for delivery)

Please send me my FREE copy of **Where to Watch Birds** and enrol me as a member of the RSPB. I enclose my 1st year's subscription of £7	
I would like to purchase _____ copies of Where to Watch Birds @ £1.50 each	
Are you a member of the RSPB ☐ Yes ☐ No	
TOTAL	

Mr/Mrs/Miss_____
(Block Capitals)
Address_____

_____
_____

_____Postcode_____

RT640

RSPB
Reg. Charity 207076

"If you were a bird you'd need protection."
Royal Society for the Protection of Birds

E

To: FAMILY CIRCLE SMOKER OFFER
Room 11, Elm House, Elm Street,
London WC1X 0BP.

8FC

Please send me _____ Brook's Original Home
Smoker(s) at £16.50 each including p&p.

I enclose cheque/PO No _____

for £_____ made payable to Standbrook
Publications Ltd.

(These rates apply to UK and BFPO only.)
Please write your name and address on the back of the
cheque and allow 28 days for delivery.

In case of any queries, please phone Brook's Home
Smokers on 0704 67068.

NAME _____

ADDRESS _____

_____

_____

F

Application Form Send Now to: The Peter Jones Collection, P. O. Box 10, Cross Street, Wakefield,
West Yorkshire WF1 3AB. Telephone (0924) 62510 or 64128
Please accept my order as follows.

Qty	Stock No.	Description	Price	P & P	Total
	1642	Caverswall 8" Plate	£19.95	£1.50	
	1641	Lion Head Beaker	£27.50	£1.00	
	1640	Loving Cup	£16.50	£1.00	
	1600	Engagement Loving Cup	£16.50	£1.00	
	6415	Minton Goblet	£70.00	£1.50	
	1886	Caernarvon Castle Rams Head Vase	£350.00	—	
	1875	St Pauls Waldenbury Rams Head Vase	£320.00	—	
	—	Two Rams Head Vases (Pair)	£650.00	—	
	1887	St. Pauls Plate	£250.00	£1.50	
	1888	Welsh Castle Plate	£35.00	£1.50	
	1889	Caernarvon Castle Mug	£15.00	£1.00	
	1861	Glamis Castle Mug	£12.50	£1.00	
	8270	Royal Worcester Garniture	£750.00	—	
	7969	Wedgwood Bell	£9.95	£0.70	

A little Bell from
Wedgwood Glass
Height 3¾" **Price**
£9.95 + 70p P & P.
A lovely 'thankyou'
present.

For orders to be despatched to Europe add £1.50
p & p per item and other countries add £3.00 p & p
per item. Price includes VAT.

Add P & P.	Total.

I enclose my chequeP.O. for £................ made payable to Peter Jones China (Mail order) Ltd or debit my Access,
Barclaycard, Trustcard, American Express, Diners Club.

Account No._____ with £_____ Signature _____

Mr/Mrs/Miss (block letters please) _____

Address_____

_____ Postcode_____

Credit Card Holders may place orders direct, day and night, seven days a week by
telephoning **Wakefield (0924) 62510** and quoting their Card number. Please ensure
the address given is that of the Credit Card holder. Reg. in England 1362134.

Practice 2   *Money: Banks, insurance and assurance*

Fill in all the forms below:

A

EasyAccess

A Halifax Xtra Interest Account still gives easy access to your money.

There is no limit to the number of withdrawals you can make as long as you give three months' notice each time. And, unlike many savings schemes of this type, you don't lose any interest.

So if you'd like to give the interest on your savings a boost, send off the coupon. Or call in at any Halifax office.

You can always rely on the world's biggest building society to give you a little extra help.

HALIFAX

Get a little Xtra help with the future.

TO: THE HALIFAX BUILDING SOCIETY, (REF IKW), PO BOX 60, TRINITY ROAD, HALIFAX HX1 2RG. Please open a Halifax Xtra Interest Account at the office nearest to my home address or at the office indicated below.

I enclose a cheque, numbered _____ for £ _____   MIN. INVESTMENT £1,000

I would like the interest to be ☐ added to the account ☐ paid to me half-yearly

Full Name(s) _____   RTX2

Address _____

_____

Signature(s) _____   Date _____

B

C

Get this coupon to us (at least 14 days before your start date) and let the NatWest Student Grant Service take care of the rest.

Mr, Mrs, Miss, Ms (Surname) _____

(Other names) _____

Home Address _____

_____ Date of Birth _____

Name of University/College _____

Course _____ Start date _____ Length of course _____

NatWest Services required (Tick box)
Servicecard (24hr cash) ☐   Cheque book and cheque card ☐   Deposit/Savings account ☐

Signature _____

National Westminster Bank Limited, Student Grant Service, FREEPOST, 41 Lothbury, London EC2B 2GN. No stamp required.

RT4

For an easier start to student life.

Practice 3   *Education application form*

Fill in the form below:

FARNLEY POLYTECHNIC	*APPLICATION FORM*

A	Surname (BLOCK CAPITALS)	
	Other Names	
	Current Address and Phone No.	
	Permanent Address	
	Date of Birth	
	Place of Birth	Age
	Marital Status	Nationality

B   Give brief details of your education:

Give brief details of any training you have received:

C   Explain your reasons for wishing to study here:

What do you hope to do after your course here?

Practice 4   *Job application form*

Fill in the form below:

Please complete this form and return it to the **Personnel Director.**

Which post are you applying for?
How did you hear about it?

Surname   Forenames Mr/Mrs/Miss

Permanent home address   Telephone

Present address (*if different from above*)   Telephone

Date of birth   Place of birth
Nationality

Marital status   Maiden name (*if applicable*)
Number of children (*sex and age*)

Name and address of next of kin (*please state relationship*)

Have you ever been employed by us before? (If so, please give details)

Practice 4 (continued)

Please list schools, colleges, universities attended

Date	Name	Subjects taken	Results

What training courses or further studies have you undertaken?

Languages (state proficiency)

Technical or professional qualifications

Give names and addresses of previous employers, working backwards from present/last job

Dates	Name and address	Salary	Job title and duties	Reason for leaving

What is your general state of health?

How much time have you had off work, through illness, in the last five years?

What are your main current interests, hobbies, membership of clubs, etc?

Names and addresses of two referees (References will not be taken up without your prior consent)

I believe the information given to be true
I understand that I may be required to undergo a medical examination

Applicant's signature   Date

FOR PERSONNEL DEPARTMENT USE

6.2 Request letters

Model

Writing to business firms and to official bodies for things is probably
the most common sort of official letter. There are two sorts of
requests you may need to make: (1) requests for goods or services;
(2) requests for information of various sorts.

   Read the letters below, and the notes on the language of request
letters following each letter.

1 Requests for goods or services.
   The following letter is a request for commercial goods:

```
The Sales Manager,                            46, Manor Way,
Transatlantic Plastics Ltd,                   Warwick,
Ventnor,                                       Warwickshire CV14 5BS
Isle of Wight
                                               28th October, 1983
Dear Sir,
         Thank you for the new Autumn catalogue received the other
day.  I would now like to order the following items from it:
         100 A4-size Mini-grip plastic bags
         4 large size pieces of plastic sheeting
I enclose a cheque for the sum of £11.80 to cover the cost of the
items and postage and packing.
I would also be very grateful if you would send me a new catalogue
every year.

              Yours faithfully,

              Robin Hopwood.

              Robin Hopwood
```

LANGUAGE NOTES

Introduction: (not usually necessary) I'm writing because / on account of ...
                                        I am writing to ...

First request: Could you (possibly) send me ...
                I'd like you to ...
                I'd be grateful if you could / would ...
                Would it be possible for you to send / sell ...
                I'd like to order ... from you / from your company.

Second request: Use the word 'also'
                 Could you also please send me / deliver ... to me ...

References to payment: I enclose/include | a cheque for £ ...
                                          | a money order for £ ...
                                          | a postal order for £ ...

116

Endings: It is not usually necessary to write any concluding sentence
such as 'I'm hoping for a speedy reply', unless this is a *second* letter of
request for the same goods or services.

2 Requests for information (factual information, explanations,
   clarifications, instructions, directions).
      The following letter is a request for information about
   emigrating to Australia:

```
                                          51 Carey Park,
                                          Torquay,
       Emigration Officer,               Devon TQ2 5BY
       Australia House,
       LONDON W1                          May 16th, 1983

       Dear Sir,

               A recent advertisement in the TV Times magazine asked
       people to consider emigrating to Australia.  I would be very
       grateful if you could give me more information about this
       possibility, particularly information about the help you offer to
       pay the cost of the fare to Australia.

       I would also like to know how one is able to become an Australian
       citizen, and how soon this could be achieved.

       The advertisement also mentioned that 'some constraints' might be
       placed on the emigration of large families.  I would be grateful
       if you could clarify precisely what is meant by 'large families'
       in this context.

               Yours faithfully,    J.J.Hunt.

               J. J. Hunt
```

LANGUAGE NOTES

Requests: I'd │ like   │ instructions/information about / directions to …
                │ appreciate │
            Could/Would you (please) │ tell me …
                                     │ explain …
                                     │ clarify … (what is meant by) …
                                     │ send me │ information …
                                     │   │ directions …
                                     │   │ instructions …
            I'd be grateful if you could tell me / send me …

Introducing new subjects: Another matter I need information on is …
                           Another point I'm not certain about is …
                           I'd *also* like some help/information/clarification
                           on …

WHAT TO DO

1 Read carefully through the two model letters, and then look at the language notes below each letter.
2 Do Practices 1 or 2 (request letters for goods or services).
   If your first practice is unsuccessful, write the other one.
   Further practice will be found on page 112 of the Teacher's Book.
3 Do Practices 3 or 4 (letters requesting information).
   If your first practice is unsuccessful, write a second one.
   Further practice will be found on page 113 of the Teacher's Book.
4 If you are happy that you are able to write both kinds of letter, you may take a test (Teacher's Book, page 114).

Practice 1

Write *one* of these letters:

A Write to a box-office (theatre/concert hall) asking for tickets to a performance.
   State: price of tickets
           place
           date
           time of day
           name of performance
   Mention payment.

B You are having trouble with your eyes. Write a letter to an optician requesting an appointment. Suggest suitable times. Inquire about payment (under National Health?).

Practice 2

Write *one* of these letters:

A You are living in a flat. The landlord has just put the rent up. You think he's put the rent up too much: write to the local Rent Officer at the Town Hall and ask him to come and fix a fair rent for your flat. Give him details of the flat and of your old and new rent.

B Write to a hotel and book a room.
   Specify: for how many people
             for how long
             arrival and departure times
             any meal requirements

Practice 3

Write *both* letters:

A Write to a language school in Britain inquiring about
   i)   summer courses, 1985   (dates/length/cost) *or*
   ii) autumn courses, 1985

B You are a carpenter and cabinet-maker. When you were in Britain
   a short while ago a Scotsman, Mr Robin Murray, asked you to
   make him a study chair, but you didn't discuss details.
      Write a letter to Mr Murray asking for precise instructions for
   construction of the chair – you know it was supposed to be a study
   chair – perhaps with a round back.
   Check: size?
           materials?
           style?
           delivery date?
           delivery address?
           payment?

Practice 4

Write *both* letters:

A You would like to take the Cambridge Proficiency Exam, but
   you're not sure exactly what the exam tests, how it tests it, when
   the exams are, how much they cost, and where you can take them.
   Write an appropriate letter to the Cambridge examinations board
   asking for information.

B You've just got a job in Britain, and, of course, you're rather
   pleased. However, you need to know certain things. You have no
   idea:
       how to get a work permit
       how to arrange your annual holidays
       how to join the health service scheme
       You'd also like to know precise directions about how to get to
       your new employers – somewhere in Norwich.
   Write a letter requesting these instructions and directions.

6.3 Letters of application

Model

Although you may never have to apply for a permanent job in Britain or America, there are other applications you may need to make: for temporary work; educational courses; cultural exchange. Sometimes the institution or company concerned will send you an application form (see Unit 6.1); but often you will be asked to submit a letter of application.

A letter of application could contain the following things:
i)   Where you got the information to make the application.
ii) Inquiries about the thing you are applying for.
iii) Your personal interests and professional experience that may make your application successful, including qualifications.

Read the following job advertisement placed in a local paper:

CANTEEN ASSISTANT

A reliable hard working person, preferably with cooking experience, is required to assist in the canteen of our modern expanding factory. Hours will be 8.30 am-2 pm, Monday-Friday. We offer excellent wages and good working conditions.

SIFAM   Please write or telephone
Personnel Manager
SIFAM
Woodland Road, Torquay
Tel: 63822 (9 a.m.-5 p.m.)

Here is an application for this job:

```
                                        10, Rowley Road,
                                        Chelston,
Personnel Manager,                      Torquay
SIFAM,
Torquay                                 18th May, 1983

Dear Sir,

        I'd like to apply for the job of 'Canteen Assistant' that I
saw advertised in yesterday's edition of the 'Post'.  For the last two
years I've been working in a Primary School canteen in Newton Abbot,
and had experience before that working in a pub.
    I'd be grateful if you could tell me what the wages and hours are
before you invite me for an interview....
```

LANGUAGE NOTES

Introduction: I'd like to apply for . . .

Job: . . . the job/post/position | advertised in . . .
| I saw advertised in . . .
| I've just seen in the . . .

. . . bursary/scholarship
. . . course/cultural exchange

Experience: (recent)
for the last . . . I've been . . .
I've been . . . since . . .

(general)
I've had experience of . . .
I've done . . . before . . .
I've never done . . . but . . .

(past)
In 1979 I worked . . .
. . . before that I worked . . .

Interests: I'm very interested in . . .   (especially interested)
I'm rather keen on . . .

One of the reasons I'm applying is . . .
One of my reasons for applying is . . .

WHAT TO DO

1 Read the advertisement for the job and the subsequent job
application letter model carefully. Look at the language notes that
follow this.
2 Do Practice 1 (applications for temporary jobs) or Practice 2
(applications for permanent jobs). If you or your teacher think you
need more practice you may find this on page 117 of the Teacher's
Book.
3 Do Practice 3 (applications for educational courses) or Practice 4
(applications for cultural visits). If you need more practice you will
find this on page 118 of the Teacher's Book.
4 There are two tests available for this unit, on page 119 of the
Teacher's Book. In these tests you will be able to choose whether to
be tested on the basis of Practices 1, 2, 3, or 4.

N.B. You may need to make a genuine application while you are
using this writing-scheme – in that case make your letter the
practice activity, and get your teacher to correct it.

Practice 1   Applications for temporary work

Write for *one* of the positions below:

A Write for the job below. Give details of age, nationality, language ability, how long you want to stay; relevant experience; relevant personal details.

SALES ASSISTANT

For busy plumbing and heating merchants. 5½ day week, £4,250 p.a. plus commission; experience in selling bathrooms, kitchens, heating, electrical for DIY in retail or wholesale essential.

Ring or write to:

Mr Newman,

D. and T. Holmes and Sons Ltd,

9 High Street,

Histon, Cambridge.

Tel: 3222.

B WAITRESSES / CHAMBERMAIDS required at Aquamarine Hotel, Brighton from May to September. Hours negotiable. Generous pay. Contact (letters only) The Manageress, Aquamarine Hotel, 14 Elm Row, Brighton SX3 5IT. Please supply references.

Apply for the temporary job above, including details of relevant experience and personality.

C CAN YOU SWIM? Earn some money this season on one of the loveliest beaches in Wales as a *lifeguard*. Apply in writing to: The Town Clerk, Town Hall, Bangor, Wales.

Apply for the summer job advertised in the *Wales Advertiser*. Give personal details; ask about wages, hours and length of season. Give possible interview times/dates.

Practice 2 *Applications for full-time jobs*

Apply for *one* of the posts advertised below.

In your letter mention:
    where you saw the ad
    why you want to apply
    previous experience
    qualifications (if any)
    your ability to speak English
    work-permit problems (if non-E.E.C. member)
Ask questions about anything you think you need to know.

PROBABLY THE MOST VARIED WORK

in our office awaits someone who enjoys typing, has a proven ability with figures and book-keeping, but wants to deal with our customers as well.

Due to continued expansion, we now want another who has these rather special talents.

If you are the right person to join us, please write in your own handwriting and tell me why.

The successful applicant will work in our small, friendly team and enjoy the working conditions and benefits which the Abbey National would be expected to offer.

BARRY CARPENTER
Abbey National Building Society
3/5 Queen Street, Newton Abbot

EVE

63 FLEET STREET, TORQUAY

Do you like beautiful clothes?

We have a vacancy for an

Attractive Person

with flair and personality for selling fashion.

Please apply in writing to Mr. J. Austin at the above address.

PART TIME/FULL TIME

ATTRACTIVE STAFF

REQUIRED.

to work in both our present Jewellery Shop in Bridge Street and/or our new jewellery/gift shop opening soon in the Garden House Hotel.

Smart appearance, and experience in jewellery and gifts an advantage, but selling ability, willingness to work under own initiative, and some flexibility of hours a MUST.

We are also looking for an

ASSISTANT WINDOW DRESSER

Apply in Writing to

KEITH LORING
6 WYNFORD WAY
CAMBRIDGE
CB4 2LB.

Practice 3   Applications for educational courses

Write applications for A or B below; C is a genuine task – do it if appropriate.

A A number of universities/polytechnics in Britain are running a one-month summer course at advanced level for the following things:

Bristol University: The Language of Nursing
                                    Commercial English
Portsmouth Polytechnic: Legal Language
                                    English for Military Advisers
                                    Advanced Translation Course
Edinburgh University: Scientific English
                                    English for the Car Industry

Write a letter of application to one of these places for one of these courses. Mention your occupational background, qualifications, experience and reasons for application.

B Look at the advert below and write a letter of application.

THE NATIONAL FILM & TELEVISION SCHOOL
INVITES APPLICANTS FOR THE COURSE
COMMENCING SEPTEMBER '83

The School announces a new programme in Production Design and additional programmes in Production, Sound and Editing.
Candidates for Writing, Directing, Camera, Design and Animation are expected to submit portfolios of supporting material.
Candidates in Production, Sound and Editing who are unable to supply supporting material may be invited to Beaconsfield for preliminary tests. The full time course occupies 3 years, but candidates already in the Industry may be accepted for shorter periods.
Closing dates for applications 28th February.
Enquiries to: NATIONAL FILM & TELEVISION SCHOOL (Dept. ST), Beaconsfield Studios, Beaconsfield, Bucks HP9 1LG Tel. (04946) 71234.

C Use your College or the public library; consult the relevant brochures, and write a letter of application to a university or polytechnic to do a 2 or 3 year course in Britain (a degree course / higher education course / H.N.D.).

Practice 4   Applications for exchange schemes

Write *one* of the letters suggested below:

A The nearest branch of the British Council has been advertising
one-month *cultural exchanges* in local papers (in your country)
recently. The idea is that someone from Britain comes and lives in
your house for a month while you go and live in theirs! Fares will
be paid by the British Council!

    Write a letter of application to the local British Council for one
of these exchanges; *explain* why an exchange would be interesting/
useful to you; *say* something about your English ability; *ask* for
more details, or about anything you're not clear about.

B
> **Work experience ! Come and work
> in the U.K. for six months or a
> year, at our expense !**
>
> The British Government are just
> beginning a scheme whereby
> exchanges may be arranged between
> *you* and someone in Britain doing
> the same job. You'll work in Britain
> while someone works in your job.
>
> Apply to : JOB SWAP
> Department for Economic Trade
> and Development
> London WC2 5TR
> Great Britain.

Write an application for the scheme, mentioning anything of
relevance, and asking for further information.

6.4   Giving information

Model

Short pieces of information are often collected by official organisations
by means of forms (see Unit 6.1). However, sometimes it's necessary
to submit/offer information which needs more space than the
typical form allows.

1 The writer of the letter below has decided to write a letter to the tax
authorities, rather than use the standard form, in order to make a clearer
statement. (N.B. Important information is still presented in *list* form.)

```
                                              Mossbank,
                                              The Drive,
                                              Culhampton,
                                              Hants WS4 1QT
          The Inland Revenue
          Winchester WS1 1PR
                                              23 August 1983


          Dear Sir,
                  I'm fairly convinced that I have been wrongly assessed for
          the current tax year, and that this wrong assessment, and
          subsequent coding, has been based on a misunderstanding of my
          earnings last year.  A statement of these follows below:
          Salary:            £11,500   (recurrent)
          Lecture Fees:        £300    (recurrent)
          Private Tuition:     £330    (non-recurrent)
          Course Fee:          £280    (non-recurrent)
          A glance at these figures should show that my coding ought to be
          based on only the first two figures, the sum of £11,800 and not on
          the higher figure of £12,410.
                              Yours faithfully,
                              G. Brownrigg
                              G. Brownrigg
```

LANGUAGE NOTES

As far as the *language* of such letters is concerned, it is almost
impossible to suggest any general formulas other than introductions:
I would like to state/inform you of/give you the following information . . .

2 When you are applying for a job or a place in an educational
institution in Britain, you may be asked to send a curriculum vitae
(known as a C.V. for short). This is a short account, laid out in a
clear form, of the details of your life. It includes the following
things:
   your name and precise address and telephone number
   your date of birth
   a precise record of schools attended
   a precise record of colleges attended
   examination qualifications
   personal achievements (e.g. in sport or music etc.)
   employment positions held (including part-time work)

interests and activities
future education plans
references (names and addresses of responsible people who will
    write a reference for you if approached)
Read the curriculum vitae below as an example:

```
CURRICULUM VITAE
Andrew Foster
105 Cheriton Road
Dorchester
Dorset  DY4 4HQ

Telephone: Dorchester (0305) 69542

Date of Birth: January 15th, 1948

Education
1953-1960  Maynard Boys Junior School, Waltham Forest, London
1960-1967  Romford Royal Liberty School, Romford, Essex
1968-1971  Hull University, Yorkshire
1974-1976  Dartington Hall, Devon
1977-1978  College of St Mark and St John, Plymouth

Qualifications
GCE 'O' level examinations (June 1965): English Language (3); English Literature
(4); Mathematics (5); Combined Science (6); History (1); Geography (1);
(December 1966): French (5).
GCE 'A' level examinations (June 1967): History (B); Economics (E);
Geography (B).

2nd Class Honours Degree in Psychology (B.Sc.) from Hull University (1971)
Diploma in Music (Dartington Hall, 1976)
Post-Graduate Certificate of Education in Primary Teaching (1978)

Other Achievements
Captain of School Swimming Team (1966-67); School Basketball Team; School
Debating Team; School Debating Vice-Captain (1967); University Basketball Team;
President of University Arts Society (1970); President of Student Union,
Dartington Hall (1975-76); Grade 8 - Piano; Grade 6 - Harpsichord.

Employment
1964-1967        Part-time work weekends/holidays furniture removal
1966-1969        Christmas work for Post Office

9/67 to 4/68     Salesman, Little Foxes Record Shop, Fulham, London
9/71 to 10/72    Salesman, HMV Record Shop, London
10/72 to 7/74    Junior Officer, Arts Council, London (with responsibility
                 for music projects)
10/76 to 6/77    Paid sabbatical president, students union, Dartington Hall
9/78 to 7/81     Teacher, Feniton Primary School, Devon (responsibility for
                 music)
9/81 to 4/83     Teacher, scale 2, Grove Middle School, Dorchester
                 (responsibility for music and language policy)
4/83             Self-employed harpsichord constructor

Interests & Activities
Playing the piano and harpsichord; playing renaissance music on authentic
instruments; instrument making, particularly keyboard instruments; chess;
European literature and philosophy; psychology; hill walking; horticulture;
active member of Ecology Party.

Personal
Married 1979
Two children, born 1981 and 1982

References
Dr Bryan Tunniwell, Dartington Hall, Devon
Mr Richard Raine, Headmaster, Grove Middle School, Dorchester, Dorset
```

Writing to companies and officials

WHAT TO DO

1 Read the notes and the models for this unit.
2 Do Practice 1. If you don't do it well enough, your teacher will ask you to repeat the task (because this is a standard piece of writing everyone should be able to do).
3 You may choose whether you want to do Practice 2 or not, and how much of it you want to do. It is divided into three parts:
A Information for visa applications.
B Information for bursaries.
C Information for residence permit applications.
4 You may take a test if you feel you can write this sort of letter. These can be found on page 121 of the Teacher's Book.

Practice 1

Imagine that you've applied for a job in Britain (pick a job/ organisation) and they have asked you to send them a curriculum vitae with the application form. Write your own version.
   Do this exercise realistically – don't make up the information.

Practice 2

Write a letter for one of following situations:

A You have applied for visas to travel in certain South American countries, and the Consulate of one of these countries has written back to you requesting information about your previous travel experience.
   Write a letter giving this information in clear and succinct form.

B The local United States Information Service office in your country has just advertised two $4,000 bursaries to any citizen in your country who wishes to travel/work for professional reasons in the United States.
   Write a letter, applying for one of these grants, stating clearly what you would use the money for, where you would go, and any other information you think might be useful.

C You have just managed to get a job in Britain, and you have applied to the Home Office for a residence permit.
   They have asked you to submit details of the job you have taken (what? how long for? where? skilled or unskilled? etc.), and also details of where you intend to live in Britain.
   Write back to the Home Office supplying this information.

6.5 Giving instructions

Model

Such letters are rather similar to letters requesting *service* (see Unit 6.2) since you normally give instructions in order to have something done. However, in such letters the writer is actually using or manipulating the service rather than requesting the use of it.

The letter below is from a woman writing to her bank and instructing them to do certain things:

```
                                                    14a The Rise
     Mr Airey                                       St Austell
     The Manager, The Midland Bank                  Cornwall CR5 4PB
     High Street
     St Austell CR1 3RU                             22/10/1983

     Dear Mr Airey,
     I have decided that it would be easier to pay a number of recurrent
     bills by bankers order; so from today, please pay the following
     amounts on the specified days:

          Addisons, High Street £25 (1st of each month)
          Co-op, St Austell £20 (10th of each month)
          Western Fuel £50 (1st of Oct/Jan/April)

     My monthly statement should be sent to the above address.

                         Yours sincerely    Maureen Brown

                         Maureen Brown
```

LANGUAGE NOTES

In such letters you can, of course, use the language of requests:
    would you / could you ... please ...
But you may also use this:
    imperative + please (please send my ...)
    X is to be done ...
    It will be necessary to ...
    X must / ought to / should be done ...
    Y mustn't/shouldn't be done ...
    I want/I'd prefer/I'd like ...

N.B. Put your own address at the top, on the right.
      Place the date underneath this.
      Put the name, position, and address of the person/organisation
      you're writing to, on the left, a little lower than your own
      address, or at the bottom of the letter below your signature.

WHAT TO DO

1 Carefully read through the model letter and the language notes that accompany it.
2 Do Practice 1. If you or your teacher feel that you need more practice, do Practice 2. Further practice can be found on page 123 of the Teacher's Book.
3 You may take a test when you feel able to write this sort of letter well. Tests will be found on page 123 of the Teacher's Book.

Practice 1

Write *one* of the following letters:

A You have just moved into a flat for a year. The landlord has said that you can have the flat decorated if you like. Write a letter to a firm of decorators you've already contacted giving *precise instructions* about the redecoration of the flat. You will be out working for most of the time the decorators will be at work.

B You need to improve your English for your rather specialised work. You have arranged with an English Language School (with an English for Special Purposes Section) to attend a course for three months. The school have just written requesting your specific instructions for the course. Reply to the school giving them such instructions. (What kind of language skills you need to develop / areas of language / degree of competence / etc.)

Practice 2

Write *one* of the following letters:

A A British couple are renting the house you own/have in your own country while you are away for six months. You do not know them. Write a letter to them giving them instructions about:
      payment of rent
      maintenance of the house
      dates of tenure
      payment of electricity/phone bills
      and anything else you think they should know

B You are planning to take a month's holiday in Great Britain, and you want to arrange travel and accommodation before you go, with a British travel agency. Write to such an agency instructing them to arrange accommodation in different places for different dates, and to obtain various transport tickets.

6.6 Letters of complaint

Model

When something offends you, causes you inconvenience, or needs
changing, in public life, it's necessary to write a letter of complaint to
the appropriate people, organisation, or department.

Read the letter below, written to the District Council, about refuse
collection (dustbins!).

```
                                              4 Larch Grove
                                              Bishop's Stortford
   Refuse Collection Dept                     CM22 4JG
   North Street
   Bishop's Stortford CM20 3TR                March 15th

   Dear Sir,
           I'm afraid that I'm forced to write to you about the collection of
   dustbins in Larch Grove.  This morning, for the third time in three weeks, the
   council dustmen have left an appalling amount of rubbish - paper, ash, cans and
   bottles - on the pavements of Larch Grove.  Surely it is not impossible to
   collect rubbish without spreading half of it over the streets.  I would be most
   grateful if you would put this matter right immediately.  We want clean houses,
   gardens, and streets in this town.
           Yours faithfully

           Geraldine Fox

   Geraldine Fox
```

LANGUAGE NOTES

Introducing the subject: I'm writing because …
          on account of …
          on the subject of …
          to draw your attention to …

Complaining: I must object …
          I must complain about …
          I find it awful / appalling / quite distressing that …
          I can no longer tolerate / bear / put up with …
          I feel something ought to be done/said … about …
          It's time that … was/were …

N.B. Put your own address at the top, on the right.
      Place the date underneath this.
      Put the name, position, and address of the person/organisation
      you're writing to, on the left, a little lower than your own
      address, or at the bottom of the letter below your signature.

WHAT TO DO

1 Read carefully through the model letter and the language notes beneath it.
2 Do Practice 1. You might find it difficult to get the tone of this sort of letter right. If necessary do Practice 2. Further practice can be found in the Teacher's Book, page 125.
3 When you feel that you can write this kind of letter quite well, you may take one of the two tests available on page 125 of the Teacher's Book.

Practice 1

Write *one* of the following letters:

A To your local council (Parks Department).
You are not very happy about the dirty beaches, water, parks in the district. Give examples. Go on to mention the problem of dogs. Have you got any tentative solutions?

B You have found that the local bookshop is inadequately stocked to serve your needs. Write to the bookshop explaining this, citing examples, and suggesting improvements.

Practice 2

Write *one* of the following letters:

A 'I'm sorry I'm late again for the meeting ... I had to wait 35 minutes for the 120 bus – that's the third time this week. When I told the conductor this he was pretty rude; I couldn't get through to the bus company office.'

'If I were you, I'd write a letter about it ... '

So, write a letter of complaint to the company.

B The *Herald Express* is the evening paper in your town. Recently however you haven't been able to read the paper because of bad printing, particularly the small ads column (paid for by customers!). Write a letter of complaint to the paper.

6.7 Letters of apology and explanation

Model

Occasionally people need to write apologies to people or
organisations for not doing something requested or promised,
or for doing it late, or for doing it poorly and inadequately. Apologies
are often made in response to 'reminders'.

Read the letter below, and notice what is being apologised for, and
how the apology is made:

```
                                    'The Vale'
                                    Uprear Avenue
        Librarian                   Troon
        Central Library
        Troon                            26.9.83

        Dear Sir,
                Thank you for your card informing me - a
        second time - that I have two books outstanding
        which are overdue.  I sincerely apologise for not
        returning Smollett's 'Humphrey Clinker' or Hardy's
        'Jude the Obscure' after your request for them; I'm
        afraid I can offer no excuse except that I forgot
        all about it.  Unfortunately, I am not in Troon
        until next Tuesday, but I will return both books on
        Tuesday afternoon.
                            Yours faithfully
                            A.L. Glover
                            Andrew Glover
```

LANGUAGE NOTES

This is an official letter so the language is relatively formal. There is
rather a small number of apology expressions available:
  I apologise for –ing . . .
  I apologise most sincerely for . . . (very formal)
  I must apologise for . . .
  I'm (very/extremely) sorry | (that) I . . .
                              | to have done . . .
                              | not to have done . . .

WHAT TO DO

1 Read carefully through the model letter and the language notes beneath it.
2 Do Practice 1. You might find it difficult to get the tone of this sort of letter right. If necessary do Practice 2. Further practice can be found in the Teacher's Book, page 127.
3 When you feel that you can write this kind of letter quite well, you may take one of the two tests available on page 127 of the Teacher's Book.

Practice 1

Write *one* of the following letters:

A A bookshop has written you the following letter:

TITLES BOOKSHOP
Fore Street
Exeter EX1 9AP

. . . .   20th November, 1983
. . . .

Dear . . . . . ,
        On checking our accounts we find that you still owe us the sum of £23.56 for books obtained and sent to you before the 4th of October. We would be most grateful if you could settle this outstanding account as soon as possible.

        Yours sincerely,

        A.L. Hoad.

        Alan Hoad (Manager)

Write an apologetic reply, enclosing payment and an explanation of prior non-payment.

B You were going to start attending an advanced English course at the Academy School in Edinburgh, Scotland, last Monday, but you've been delayed. Write a letter of apology and explanation.

Write *one* of the following letters:

A You have been given a job in a hotel, but your future employers
first want to see your professional certification. They write you this
letter:

Queen's Hotel 2, STATION ROAD, CAMBRIDGE CB4 2JY

```
---------
---------                                    24 May 1983

Dear -------,

            I'm afraid we still haven't

received copies of your professional diplomas

promised us at the time of your interview, on

the 6th of May.  Unfortunately we cannot

employ you until these are forthcoming.


            Yours very sincerely,

            Richard Adamson

            R. A. ADAMSON   (Personnel Officer)
```

B You are a craftsman/woman in your own country. You have
promised to supply the 'Owl and the Pussycat' shop with a number
of items (furniture/pottery/toys/jewellery etc.). Unfortunately, you
haven't made these things yet. Write a letter of apology and
explanation to the shop.

Section 7 Presenting facts, ideas and opinions

Introduction

Other sections in this book are concerned with describing experience (Section 4) and reporting experience (Section 5). This section is mostly concerned with *discussing* experience, which involves evaluation and comment. It should be obvious that to do this successfully you need also to be able to describe and report experience; so, successful work in this section may depend upon being able to do the sorts of writing practised in Sections 4 and 5.

This section should give you practice in writing down your ideas and feelings, or other people's ideas or feelings, about aspects of life (factually based or abstract ideas).

LANGUAGE NOTES

To be able to do this sort of expository writing successfully you will need a lot of organisational skills. This involves the linguistic ability to:

express ideas in sentences   (write complex sentences)
develop ideas in texts   (link sentences together and sequence them)
qualify and modify ideas and information

Are you able to use the following language?
i)   Relative words (who, what, which, whose).
ii) Words that join two (complete) parts of a sentence: for time (when, as), place, reason, cause, contrast (although, even if), hypothesis (if).
iii) Words that link a sentence to the one before it: to sequence (first, after that), to add, to contrast, to summarise.
iv) Words that join facts and ideas (that, this, such).
v)   Words and phrases that introduce comments by the writer on attitude towards what is written or the style in which it is written (frankly, to put it in a nutshell).
Your teacher will help you with these skills.

● This section covers the following areas:
7.1 Writing paragraphs – the basic unit for discussing ideas and experience is usually considered to be the paragraph.
7.2 Writing letters to newspapers in order to explain, comment upon and complain about things.
7.3 Writing summary reports. Long arguments, discussions, reports or speeches sometimes have to be made shorter for professional and personal reasons: to save space, to become more precise and more readable.

136

7.4 Writing personal and factual reports.

7.5 Writing essays. This is the writing of extended and developed ideas; you will probably only need to attempt this unit if you need to write essays in a university context or for high level English examinations.

Remember: The practices in this section are all based on real-life situations which require a written communication between two *English-speaking* people. Thus, when a task suggests that you write to a friend, acquaintance or organisation, it means an English-speaking person or organisation.

7.1 Paragraph writing

Model

A paragraph is a unit of information unified by a central, controlling idea or theme.

This central idea is often expressed at some point in the paragraph by one sentence (the main sentence). This sentence is most frequently found at the beginning of the paragraph, but can come at the end or even in the middle of the paragraph.

Example 1   (main sentence comes first)

The balance of payments in Greece last year was less favourable than the Government expected. There was a 3.9 billion dollar trade gap, consumer prices increased around 13% rising to 14% in the last months, and wage increases this year are expected to top 20%; the growth of the Gross National Product in 1977 was down to 3.5%. In addition per capita productivity in Greece is running at only one-third the CECD average, according to its latest report. Industrial development in Greece is also near the bottom of the organisation's league. Thus the gap is likely to stay for a little while . . .

Example 2   (main sentence is sometimes found in the middle or at the end)

The view was beautiful and the weather at its balmiest. I was mildly surprised at the warmth of the evenings. The hotel surpassed itself in its food, and I don't think I've ever tasted better trout. The golf course had been meticulously cared for and one rarely seemed to meet anyone else on it. *Portcudden, I feel, is thus a place to be recommended for anyone who wishes to stay at a place off the normal tourist track.*

137

A paragraph usually *develops* an idea – that is, it adds information, explanation, examples and illustrations to the central theme or idea until the theme is fully developed, and there's nothing more to say which is essential.

Example 3   (developing a central idea)

I'm fascinated by my Swedish grandmother; by her increasing age, by her wholehearted scepticism and lack of sentimentality, and above all, by her abiding interest in the kings and queens of Europe! She's about 92 now, I forget, but seems never to require the services of a doctor; or, in some way mysterious to me, has ceased to believe in illness. She's ceased to believe in a lot of things, including festivity, news, success, money, the efficacy of postal services, and heaven. What she does still believe in is the royal blood of the deposed kings and queens of Greece, Yugoslavia, and Russia.

The rest of the paragraph generally expands the theme contained in the main sentence, and each idea round the controlling theme or idea is supported by information and evidence (in the form of illustrations and examples), and by argument.

Look at the diagram of this, and then read the example below:

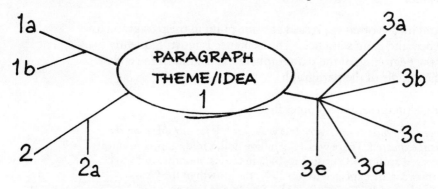

1   The material advantages of life in Paris make a ludicrous comparison
1a   with existence in Portuguese rural areas. The Fonsecas, an emigrant
      family from a village near the northern border now have a two-storey
      house, a garage with a Citroen in it, a stereo and a colour television.
2   He works as a foreman in a car factory, she as a cook in the university.
2a   Between them they make nearly £2,000 a month, enough to send their
      two daughters to private school. For their four weeks paid holiday they
1b   can drive back to Portugal to see their neighbours still living in houses of
3a   mud and slate built in the last century. Some have no chimneys and
3b   smoke billows out of the front door at meal times. The lugubrious oxen
      who pull the carts live in the room downstairs; hay and vegetables are
3c   loaded in the lofts. Some villagers have no telephone or electricity. Many
3d   more have no water other than a well. A few have only a steep dirt track,
3e   impassable in winter, to connect them to the outside world.

1   Main sentence – Comparison of Paris life with Portuguese rural life
1a Illustration (the Fonsecas)
2   Life in Paris – jobs
2a Earnings from jobs
1b Return from modern Paris to old-fashioned Portugal
3a Undeveloped rural Portugal – illustration
3b Illustration
3c Illustration
3d Illustration
3e Illustration

Writing good, clear, well-organised paragraphs also depends on the ability to (1) order ideas/facts (2) summarise (3) state reasons, conclusions and connections (4) qualify statements of fact or ideas.

Any good writing requires good paragraph-writing, but it is particularly important when writing expositions of states, feelings and phenomena; in stating arguments, and engaging in written debate. Thus most of the practice for 7.1 will be in these areas.

WHAT TO DO

1 Study the model very carefully.
2 It may be important for you to do the two exercise types which are to be found in the Teacher's Book on page 131. If you don't have the Teacher's Book, ask your teacher for the exercises, one at a time.
  Exercise 1 is to help you identify the main idea in paragraphs.
  Exercise 2 is designed to help you build up paragraphs on your own from instructions.
3 Do Practice 1. This is writing paragraphs from a main idea.
  If you need more practice do Practice 2, or Extra Practice 1 in the Teacher's Book page 134.
4 Do Practice 3. This allows you to write a paragraph from a list of topics given to you. If you need more practice, do Practice 4, or Extra Practice 2 in the Teacher's Book on page 134.
5 When you think you can write good paragraphs, take a test (Teacher's Book page 135).

Practice 1

In this practice you will be given main sentences and you must write a paragraph around them.

Write *two* of the following suggested paragraphs:

A Write a 90–100-word paragraph *beginning* with the main sentence:

'The British attitude to dogs is difficult to understand . . . '

B Write a 90–100-word paragraph *containing* this main sentence:

'X is / is not a place I would want to live in for a long time.'

C Write a 90–100-word paragraph *beginning* with the main sentence:

'It is difficult to say whether meetings between two or more countries on the sports field does more for international harmony, or for international aggression.'

D Write a 90–100-word paragraph *ending* with this main sentence:

i) 'This proves that women are not meant to be in powerful, responsible positions.'

or

ii) 'This shows that it is about time women shared in the world's decision-making processes.'

Practice 2

Write *two* of the following suggested paragraphs. Concentrate on making your writing accurate and expressing your ideas as clearly and as logically as possible – try to be interesting.

A Write a 90–100-word paragraph *beginning* with the main sentence:

'The way the English treat their children is very different from/ similar to . . . '

B Write a 90–100-word paragraph *ending* with the main sentence:

'I'm afraid I didn't like the film at all, and wouldn't recommend it.'

C Write a 90–100-word paragraph *containing* the main sentence:

'The British Sunday is essentially a day of rest and indolence.'

D Write a 90–100-word paragraph *containing* the main sentence:

'My teenage years were / have been a very happy/confused/ miserable period in my life ... '

Practice 3

This practice is for free paragraph writing. Choose *one* of the subjects below:

N.B. Your paragraph should be clearly on one idea, perhaps stated somewhere by a main sentence. It should develop logically, and clearly.

A Write a 90–100-word paragraph on 'Shyness'.

B Write a 90–100-word paragraph on 'Anger'.

C Write a long paragraph on 'Fashions'.

Practice 4

This practice is for free paragraph writing.
Choose *one* of the subjects below:

A Write a 90–100-word paragraph on 'Patience'.

B Write a 90–100-word paragraph on 'Jealousy'.

C Write a long paragraph on 'Prisons'.

7.2 Letters to newspapers

Model

People write letters to newspapers for many reasons, but the majority of 'Letters to the editor' fall into the following categories:

1 Letters that comment on and add information to articles written in the newspaper/magazine.
2 Letters that comment on and add information to generally newsworthy events.
3 Letters that support or argue against views expressed in the newspaper/magazine by journalists or other readers' letters.
4 Letters that complain about (or, less often, commend) something, and suggest changes/improvements.

The letters below illustrate these four general functions.

1 Thinking big when doing wrong

Sir,—An essential lesson for all aspiring criminals was contained in two separate reports in the Guardian of September 26.

The first reported that three former directors of the Birmingham company C. Bryant and Son, involved in corruption netting them £112 millions worth of contracts, had had their sentences reduced, in one case from four years to 12 months. The second report told of the gaoling of three members of a bag snatching gang (who happened to be black), in one instance for three years.

The moral is, think big. And, if you must get caught, make sure you are judged by your peers.—Yours,

M. F. Rennard.
35 Millfield Road,
York.

2 Living standards

WOULD it not be useful to standardise seat belts on all makes of cars, as they do on the Continent ?

My parents were recently involved in a car crash and one of the first people on the scene was the driver of a rescue vehicle who asked them how to release their seat belts when his own attempts failed.

If my parents had been unconscious or the car on fire there might have been fatal consequences.

(Miss) WENDY WRIGHT,
West Witton,
Leyburn,
North Yorkshire.

3 Fairer savers

YOUR report of new cheap fares to be introduced by British Caledonian between Gatwick and Glasgow and Edinburgh, compares them with Second Class single rail fares between London and Scotland and suggests only a small differential.

This is not, however, a fair basis of comparison. A truer one would be a comparison with our own Big City Saver fares between London and Scotland. On this basis, for the return journey, rail is no less than £25 cheaper.

P. A. KEEN,
Chief Passenger Manager,
British Railways Board,
Marylebone Road,
London, N.W.

4

Why does the PO take so long to pass the parcel?

Sir,—I have missed the last posting date for surface mail to reach New Zealand by Christmas ; it was October 9—earlier than last year, which in turn was earlier than the year before.

Can it really take 11 weeks for mail to reach New Zealand? In the 1840s whole families emigrated with their trunks, etc., and took only six weeks to get there. What explanation can the Post Office offer ? — Yours sincerely,

M. BLACKBURN.

Newcastle-upon-Tyne.

PS. I posted in good time last year, but not one parcel arrived before mid-January.

It is quite possible to write a very excited letter to a newspaper, but it's probably more effective to write coolly, dispassionately, and articulately. Arguments should be explained coolly, and clearly; evidence should be presented precisely.

Look at letter (1). The writer obviously feels very strongly about the different punishments handed out to criminals from a different class, but he makes his point more powerfully and clearly by *not* getting excited – by placing the two essential facts side by side, and letting them speak for themselves; the writer also uses irony rather well.

LANGUAGE NOTES

It is not possible to say what language one needs to write such letters; it depends upon the subject.

However, make sure you know how to do the following things:
– order ideas/evidence
– summarise ideas/facts/evidence
– compare and contrast
– introduce countering arguments
– introduce evidence and illustration
– describe cause and effect
– make conclusions

WHAT TO DO

1 Read the four models and the notes that explain them. Also look carefully at the language notes. Your teacher will give you help and advice if you need it.
2 Do Practice 1. You might find that you need to do more practice. If so, do Practice 2. Further practice can be found in the Teacher's Book on page 137.
3 Do Practice 3. This is a more demanding sort of practice, which asks you not only to react to something, but to produce reasoned arguments in response to someone else's ideas or opinions.
4 When you feel that you can write these sorts of letters quite effectively, ask to take a test (Teacher's Book, page 138).

Practice 1

Write *two* of the letters to newspapers suggested below:

A You find it quite pleasant to live in Britain, particularly in your town or city. However, you find a lot of things are dirty, or vandalised. Write a mild letter of complaint to the local newspaper.

B Read the letter asking for advice, and the reply offering advice. Then write a letter arguing for or against the advice given. Make sure your arguments are reasonable and well illustrated with points from the letter.

He ignores me

My husband retired recently and thinks of nothing but his garden. He ignores me all day, and most nights he's at the pub with like-minded friends. At home we hardly talk to each other, and I'm going out of my mind with boredom and loneliness. But how can I wrench his mind away, for one second, from his precious roses and beans?

Please don't think of wrenching him away from anything – it's a bossy attitude, and impossible anyway. You can't stifle someone's urge to grow things, any more than you can stop things growing. But what I'd like to know is what, if anything, you like to make grow? There must be something you can nurture – friendships, a hobby, your home, cooking (with all those delicious, fresh vegetables), flower arranging – instead of all this resentment against your husband's enjoyment of his gardening. A productive garden is a plus for both of you, and I'm sure you'd see it that way if you had some creative outlets of your own.

C Read the article and write a letter commenting on it

White exodus grows

HARARE: A record number of whites joined the exodus from Zimbabwe in September.

During the month, 1,776 left and only 286 entered the country, producing a record net loss of 1,490.

And the last three months of this year are expected to be higher.

White civil servants are expected to boost the emigration figures dramatically, as they leave before the advent of black rule.

At the present rate, the white exodus for the year is expected to reach up to 20,000.

Practice 2

Write *two* of the letters to newspapers suggested below:

A Read the editorial arguing the need for more and different financing for health care in Britain, and write a letter to the editor, commenting on it.

> The Health Service does need more cash. It is not going to get it from general taxation with the economy still sluggish and uncompetitive. So other forms of finance have got to be found.
>
> Old charges for prescriptions will have to be increased. New ones for food and l a u n d r y in hospital will have to be imposed. The charitable instincts of the public will have to be tapped by the hospitals at local level. And the Government will have to nurture, not restrict, the growth of private health insurance.
>
> *It is emotive escapism to moan about the state of the Health Service if we are not prepared to will the m e a n s to improve it.*
>
> What is the use of h a v i n g a 'caring' Government if its political principles remain too n a r r o w to permit it to examine and exploit fresh ways of raising funds to care adequately for the ill, the infirm and the old ?

B Pick a subject/theme which has been in the news during the last week (in newspapers / on radio / on TV), and write a letter to one of the British national newspapers on the subject.

145

C This letter was written to the Editor of the Oxford evening
newspaper. Read it, and write a letter, supporting or attacking it

```
                                            5, Dean Road,
                                            Oxford,
                                            Oxon OX9 3SP

   Editor,                          28th November, 1983
   Herald Express,
   Oxford OX1 3AP

   Dear Sir,

        Am I alone in thinking that despite the
   foreign cash they bring in, foreign students do
   not improve the character of Oxford - being
   usually, dirty, noisy, and very bad-mannered....
```

Practice 3

Here are two letters on serious subjects both written to newspapers.
Write a letter to the editor, commenting on or arguing for or against
all or part of *one* of these letters:

A   Sir,—Nationwide (BBC-1, November 30) featured a debate on vandalism which demonstrated its extensive financial and social cost. Two alternative approaches were debated.

One favoured vigilantes to patrol cities; the other preferred good technical design and colourful appearance of objects, which have been found to reduce attack. While some vandalism is mindless, much of it is combined with stealing money; principal targets are telephone boxes, parking meters and, in some places, bus conductors and gas meters.

A fairly simple solution has been put forward from time to time, and it is astonishing that the authorities fail to get together on this. Instead of putting money into these various gadgets, one should be able to buy in advance booklets of tickets for standard denominations of 5p, 10p, 50p, etc to use for a wide variety of purposes, including the London Underground system. As the ticket is inserted into the machine, it is cancelled and therefore no good to a thief.

It would save the long queues on one-man buses and the Underground, and a great deal of senseless labour in collecting coins and constantly adapting machines

Instead of using such a simple method for a large variety of uses, our mindless bureaucrats invent gimmicks like a special plastic card to insert into telephone machines — and nothing else.

(Dr) **Frank A. Heller.**
The Tavistock Institute of Human Relations,
London NW3.

B

£46 TV licences: the old, old story of the honest paying for the rest

Sir,—The BBC's current application to raise the colour TV licence fee from £30 to £46 appals me. To begin with, this is over a 50 per cent increase which no commercial firm would be allowed to charge for its services, but which apparently a Government sponsored monopoly is allowed to do.

It was recently announced in the House of Commons that the latest figures show that 96 per cent of households have a television set and it is a pity that we cannot have the latest figures of how many of the 96 per cent have taken out television licences. I should be surprised if the figure exceeded 75 per cent.

TV licences seem to me to be largely a matter of conscience which does not rate very highly. I know that the Post Office keeps some kind of check on newly purchased sets but what of all those which were bought before this check came into being ?

I don't think many people take the threat of the detector vans seriously as there are so few of them and few people have ever seen one, so they are no deterrent to the licence evader. The chances of being caught by one must be one in a million. So the honest citizens who take out their TV licences are subsidising the dodgers who do not.

The only remedy would be to have a television levy, as advocated recently by an MP. A levy would be set at a mean figure to cover both black-and-white and colour—in any case before long all TV sets will be in colour. I am sure that the four per cent who do not have television would not complain at having to suffer a little as they do in the case of rates where they pay for many services and amenities which they never use. The levy could be collected through the income tax or the rates or some similar method without much trouble and paid over to the BBC. Finally could not pensioners be allowed a reduced fee? — Yours faithfully.

Paul Lund

Cheadle Hulme,
Cheadle,
Cheshire.

7.3 Summary reports

Model

You'll need to write summaries when you want to convey information to someone (either for official or personal reasons) in a condensed form.

The object in writing a summary is to express the basic meanings of a longer piece of information without losing any essential information, or clarity; and without changing the emphasis of the original information.

Writing effective, clear summaries can involve using language which is different from the language of the original – but not necessarily.

USES

1 You may read an interesting article and want to write to someone about this article, describing the main points.
2 You may need to convey information to someone from sources such as:
    i)   official documents
    ii)   laws
    iii) house/job advertisements
    iv)   plans
    v)   brochures/prospectuses
3 You may need, either officially or informally, to report some sort of speech (an argument / a meeting). Not every word is important – you need to report the main points.

TECHNIQUE

When you write a summary remember the following points:
1 Go through each part of the source information and note what is important/essential.
2 Decide whether any details are also important.
3 Exclude unimportant details, anecdotes, personal comments, examples, illustrations, data etc.
4 Write out the basic ideas as simply as possible. You may have to reword them.

Below, on the left, there is an extract from an article on a successful career. On the right, there are some notes on the main ideas. Underneath the article you'll find a brief summary.

Where and how to cut your losses

Half the skill in getting ahead on the career front is knowing when to move on. In everyone's life there comes a moment when they should make the break – the world is full of has-beens who, perhaps, just didn't have the courage to take a chance when that chance came. It pays to constantly re-assess where you stand. A good stock question to ask yourself is "Where am I going to be, this time next year, if I stay in the same job?" Each career has a different kind of time-scale. The sales scene moves fast – you tend to make your money in the early years, then move on to management before you are too old and too tired to continue with the foot-in-the-door technique and the patter. The same thing goes, to a certain extent, for advertising. But other careers move at a different pace – to become head curator in a museum, for instance, or head librarian, may take years.

important to know
 when to change jobs

many miss the
 right moment

try to consider your
 position a year ahead

some {careers
 {jobs move slowly,
 some fast

Summary

In this article on successful careers it says that it's important to know when to change jobs. Many people miss the right moment; so you should always think about where you are now, and where you'll be in a year. Some jobs, though, move slowly, while others move quickly – careers have different time-scales.

Below there is an advertisement for a house. Notes on the essential information have been made to the right of the advertisement. Underneath you'll find a short summary.

PHILIP YOUD & IRVING
Estate Agents and Surveyors

13 HYDE ROAD, PAIGNTON. TELEPHONE 523460

PICK OF THE WEEK

KINGSWEAR — Set amidst half an acre of its own wooded gardens is this spacious Detached Bungalow of timber frame construction in the delightful village of Kingswear on the River Dart. Magnificent views over the surrounding rolling countryside. Large lounge, 2 double bedrooms, kitchen, bathroom and w.c. Garage, ample room for extension and for caravan/boat, etc. A truly delightful property within easy reach of the village. Offers invited in excess of **£50,000**. Apply Sole Selling Agents as above.

bungalow in Kingswear
½ acre of wooded garden
good views
2 big bedrooms, 1 lounge
garage - lots of space
over £50,000

Summary

I've got an advert here for a 2-bedroom / 1 lounge bungalow near Kingswear. It's got good views, and ½ an acre of wooded garden. There's a garage and lots of space. The price is over £50,000.

WHAT TO DO

1 Read the two models. They show a text and notes on the main points in the text. Below each text is a summary. Study these carefully.
2 Do Practice 1. More practice is available on page 141 of the Teacher's Book. Model summaries can be found on page 168 of the Teacher's Book.
3 Do Practice 2. More practice is available on page 142 of the Teacher's Book. You will find model summaries on page 169 of the Teacher's Book.
4 If you are interested, Practice 3 gives practice in summarising speech and discussion. More practice is available on page 143 of the Teacher's Book. The Teacher's Book also offers model summaries on page 169.
5 When you feel confident about writing summaries, ask your teacher for a test (page 144 of the Teacher's Book).

Practice 1

You write summary reports, both formally, and informally in letters
when you wish to inform someone of the basic contents of an
informational item. Practices 1 and 2 concern summaries of
arguments, opinions, and contentious events.

Write *both* A and B:

A Read the short letter, written by a reader to a woman's magazine;
then write a summary sentence, 12–15 words long.

Not a patch?

You can make inexpensive,
washable, pretty and easy patches
and pockets for a toddler's worn
dungarees from the pages of cloth
story books. They'll lengthen
its life, too.—Gwyneth
Zambonini, Harpenden, Herts.

B Read the report. Notice that there are five things to summarise:
i)   the event
ii) the context of the event
iii) Norwegians' reaction to event
iv) Norwegian press reaction
v)   British reaction to Norwegian reaction
Using these ideas write a 60–80-word summary of the article.

Princess shocks Norwegians

By Gareth Parry

Many Norwegians were
shocked and wrote to the newspapers when Princess Anne—
President of the Save the
Children Fund—was shown on
television snubbing a five-year-
old while visiting a hospital
nursery in Oslo at the weekend.
But a Buckingham Palace spokesman said last night that the
impression gained was "totally
untrue," and was the result of
the film being edited and "taken
out of context."

The Princess, in Norway for a
fund-raising day for a national
children's charity, appeared on
television on Sunday night. When
five-year-old Oeyvind Stroem
tried to shake hands with her,
he appeared to have been
spurned. "No cuddle, not even a
smile. . . " the Dagbladet newspaper bannered on its front
page.

The media said it received
"thousands" of phone calls object-
ing to the Princess's manner and
suggesting that she should "go
home." Norway's largest circula-
ting newspaper, Verdens Gang,
said that most of its callers
asked how a Princess, who was
a mother herself, could show
such coolness towards a child.

A spokesman for Princess
Anne said last night : "The television clip was taken out of
context and gave a totally untrue
impression."

151

Summary-writing is a difficult art and involves excellent, accurate reading ability as well as writing skills. Don't be surprised if your teacher suggests you do another practice. There are model answers on page 167 of the Teacher's Book.

Practice 2

Write *both* A and B:

A Read the short passage below about safety; then write a 20–30-word sentence summarising the passage.

> The way I see it, people need to be made far more aware of safety in ordinary everyday situations—a classic example, of course, is the child reaching for the bottle of tablets Mum forgot to lock away—and it seems to me that the cinema would be the ideal place in which to get the message across. A film about safety tucked at the end of the forthcoming attractions and advertisements would then be seen by a large section of the population.

B Below you'll find an article called 'The way I see it'. Go through each of the seven paragraphs and decide what point each is making. Write this in note form for yourself.

> N.B. Some paragraphs contain more essential information than others – some paragraphs may have nothing to add, or may merely repeat some information.

When you have written your notes, write them up into a 90–100-word summary. There are model answers on page 168 of the Teacher's Book.

The way I see it

Please, Mr. Taxman, help us working mums

One of the great injustices of our tax system is that no allowance can be claimed by working mothers on wages they must pay someone to care for their children while they are working.

In my case, I have a local lady who picks up my child from school, brings her home, gives her tea and stays with her until my return. For this service I pay £10 a week. Without it, I could not go out to work at all.

Before I found this "treasure" I had two foreign au pair girls. The first one got the sulks and ate like an elephant; the second was delightful, well worth her wages plus her keep—until we got our phone bill, which was £100 higher than usual!

Can I claim an allowance for this "hidden" cost

of working? Silly question. Of course I can't.

If a mother has children under five years of age, the problem is different. She needs full-time care for her kids and she may, if she's lucky, find a State nursery to do the job. For children of school age, though, there is no such provision, and if a mother wants her children collected from school and cared for till she comes home—well, she must pay for the privilege.

If she cannot afford to do so, her kids will probably become latch-key kids—belonging to that "lost" generation who go home to empty houses where there's no-one to hear about their day. Worse, they might not even bother to go home at all, but hang about instead, getting up to all kinds of mischief.

We can claim an allowance for looking after an elderly relative, so why not an allowance on money we have to pay out in order to get our kids looked after? For many mums, working is not a luxury—it's a necessity.

Practice 3

Before you do this practice, it will be useful to do Unit 5.4 (reporting speech).

This practice is about summarising discussions and speeches.

Do *both* A summarising a discussion informally and
         B summarising a speech formally.

A Two English acquaintances of yours have the following discussion. In writing a letter to another English friend, include a summary of their discussion. (A model answer to this will be found in the Teacher's Book, page 168.)

Kate: You use much too much salt on your food, Paul – it's not at all good for you!

Paul: Why on earth not! If you didn't have salt on your food it would taste awful . . . like eating cardboard or sand . . . just imagine bread without salt in it, or potatoes or pasta cooked without salt!

Kate: But too much salt is bad for you . . . it causes high blood pressure and later on, heart-attacks—

Paul: But I don't have high blood pressure—

Kate: Let me finish – it also disguises the tastes of food, the real tastes . . . which are much more subtle than salt, and which we have lost the sensitivity to appreciate any more.

Paul: I really don't agree . . . traditionally people have thought that salt brings out the flavour of food rather than masks it.

Kate: Maybe for some things, but why don't you just try less salt and see?

153

B On 9 July, 1982 a man got into the Queen's bedroom in
   Buckingham Palace without anyone seeing him. The Home
   Secretary, Mr Whitelaw, now Viscount Whitelaw, asked Mr
   Dellow to hold an inquiry into this breakdown of security for the
   Queen. Below you can read part of Mr Whitelaw's report to the
   House of Commons. Make a concise summary of it. (A model
   answer will be found on page 168 of the Teacher's Book.)

   Mr W.: Mr Dellow's inquiry has revealed that although there were
           technical failures, the basic cause of the breakdown of security
           was a failure by the police to respond efficiently and urgently.
           Furthermore, the incident revealed slackness and weakness in
           supervision. The Commander 'A' District has resigned from the
           (police) force and the Chief Inspector at the Palace has been
           transferred to other duties. These were the two officers charged
           with the supervision of the uniformed officers at the Palace. Mr
           Dellow has also outlined the serious errors and omissions which
           exposed the Queen to danger. As a result, four other police
           officers are subject to disciplinary inquiries. One of these officers
           has been suspended and two have been removed from their
           former duties. I am sure that the House (of Commons) will
           accept that the officers concerned have a right to a fair hearing. I
           must remind the House that I have an appellate responsibility in
           police discipline cases; and it is not proper for me to comment
           further on these individual cases.

7.4 Personal and factual reports

Model

You usually need to write reports in order to convey clearly to other people an account of an experience you've had, whether of things (food/furniture/beer! etc.), or people, education, social activities, and so on, so that they may then or in the future know whether it is worth undertaking the same experience. For example: (a) A company who send a student on an English course may want him to write a report on it so that other people may see if the course is valuable for them. (b) A tourist office may need to write a report on various facilities available in its town, so that foreign tourists find out what is available. (c) A teacher may be asked to write a reference (personal report) on a student.

Normally most of these reports would be written in your own language, but where there are multi-lingual considerations, or tourism for example, this will need to be done in English. At any rate, it is hoped that all the practices for 7.4 will involve you in fairly realistic exercises.

Below are examples of three different types of written report:

REPORT ON A PERSON

To whom it may concern: <u>Personal Reference for Mr Jean Tironez</u>

I've tutored Jean Tironez for the last two months at the English Centre, Bristol, and I've been in intermittent contact with him for the last five months, since January. Throughout this time he has been a hard-working, enthusiastic student of English, clearly motivated by the desire both to learn more English for his personal satisfaction, and also to participate more fully and more intelligently in British life.

Mr Tironez's <u>speaking ability</u> is fairly good, though he still needs to do some intensive work on word pronunciation; his <u>written skills</u> are of the highest order, and show a sensitivity to the requirements of different functional purposes. He has worked very thoroughly at the receptive skills: his <u>reading ability</u>, partly the result of his wide reading outside the classroom, is excellent; his <u>listening ability</u> is not yet close enough to what might be expected of him at a very high level of discourse, but is adequate enough to allow him to follow detailed lectures, and to participate in seminars.

As a student he has been a delight to teach, both in the attention he has paid to his own studies, and the generous help he has frequently offered to those around him; and this generosity has always been set off by a Gallic charm and the occasional flash of true wit - all of which ensures that this reference can be nothing less than glowing.

REPORT ON A CHESS MEETING

Leonard Barden
Chess

LAST MONTH'S Benedictine international at the Wythenshawe Forum was the first master event in Manchester since the tournament of 1890 won by Dr Tarrasch, world title candidate and one of the greatest chess writers. With three grandmasters and two international masters, the Benedictine carried the possibility of FIDE title norms, though none was achieved.

Two features emerged from the results. One was the high class of play of the young French champion, Aldo Haik, who reeled off eight successive wins, then drew his remaining games to finish two points clear. It was appropriate that Haik should score his best international result in a tournament sponsored by the makers of the famous French liqueur. Judged on his form in Manchester and other successes like the Aaronson Masters earlier this year, he could become France's first native-born grandmaster.

The other notable feature was the very good results of the North of England and Manchester players against the masters. Richard Britton, aged 21, of Sheffield University, tied for second prize with GM Jansa (Czechoslavakia) while Chris Baker, 20, of Coventry, shared fourth with GM Forintos (Hungary) and Rind (USA).

REPORT ON A CLASSICAL GUITAR COURSE

I attended this course throughout the winter from October 25th to the end of March, 16 lessons in all, each two and a half hours long.

The course was run by two tutors, who took it in turns to teach a month at a time, the first spending four weeks on guitar technique, and the second on the learning of particular pieces. Some of the early practical work was rather too simple for some of the course participants and some course members felt that this session was rather wasted. The study of pieces by Villa-Lobos was felt to be well worthwhile.

One major criticism might well be that selection criteria were not strict enough, and that standards varied too much....

LANGUAGE NOTES

When your report concerns a sequence/series of events you may need sequencing and narrative skills (see 5.3).

You will certainly need clear, objective descriptive skills, perhaps of people (see 4.1), of human scenes and events (see 4.4 and 5.1), and of places (see 4.2).

You will also need the ability to make balanced judgements and criticisms.

WHAT TO DO

1 Read the explanatory notes for this unit. Then read the three models.
2 Do Practice 1. If you or your teacher are not happy with your work, do Practice 2. Further practice is available on page 147 of the Teacher's Book.
3 Now go on to Practice 3. If you need to do more practice, do Practice 4. Further practice is available on page 148 of the Teacher's Book.
4 Tests for the unit are available on page 149 of the Teacher's Book, when you think that you are able to write good reports.

Practice 1

Write *one* item from A and *one* from B:

A REPORTS ON FACILITIES

  i) Write a report on the shopping facilities available in your town or village. Include comments on variety, prices, opening hours, service, payment procedures. (This report will be read by foreign tourists.)

  ii) Write a report on the educational and recreational facilities available to you at your place of work, for the benefit of future colleagues.

B REPORTS ON PEOPLE

  i) Write a report on a boss you once had or still have. This is not a character-study but a report on a man/woman *as a boss*. Mention authority, tact, efficiency, handling of staff etc.

  ii) Write a report on a landlady you've had or still have. You should concentrate on this person *as a landlady*, commenting on things such as her efficiency, warmth, ability to get on with her lodgers etc.

Practice 2

Write *one* report from A and *one* report from B:

A REPORTS ON FACILITIES

i) Write a report (for British people coming to your country) on the transport facilities in your town or village. Mention bus services (cost, frequency, comfort, etc.); train services (services to other towns and cities, comfort, speed); taxi services and also air services if appropriate.

ii) Write a report on English food based on the food and drink you've consumed in homes and in pubs and restaurants. Include comments on variety, frequency, cost, English attitudes to food.

B REPORTS ON PEOPLE

i) Write a report on a teacher you've had at any time in your life. This is not necessarily a portrait of the teacher – but a report on him/her *as a teacher*. It needn't necessarily be a good teacher. Suggestions: enthusiasm, efficiency, thoroughness, rapport.

ii) Write a report on a colleague you've had at any time in your life – or a fellow student. Write about the colleague *as a working colleague*. Write about the fellow student *as a student*.

Practice 3

Write *one* report from A and *one* from B:

A REPORTS ON EVENTS

i) Write a report on a day-long wine-tasting festival you went to recently. Report on what happened during the day, the official programme of events; the uses and success of the festival etc.

ii) Write a review of a play you went to recently. Comment on the play itself (this may involve use of description and narrative), the acting, staging, and audience reactions.

B REPORTS ON COURSES/JOBS/PROJECTS

i) Write a report on any course of professional training you may have done at some time in your life. Mention factual details, and also methods of training, success and failure of training etc.

ii) Write a report on the complete course you've been attending while studying English. Talk about the implicit intentions, methods, surprises, difficulties, successes.

Practice 4

Write *one* report from A and *one* from B:

A REPORTS ON EVENTS

i) Recently you spent a morning at a fashion show or a motor show. Write a report on how the show was organised, on what you saw, on whether things could have been done in a different or better way, and include your general impressions of the morning.

ii) For the benefit of future students attending your English course, write a detailed report on the programme of social events that was arranged for the students. This will involve description and comment.

B REPORTS ON COURSES/JOBS/PROJECTS

i) Write a report on the nature of your present job: the tasks involved, the skills required, the sources of problems, and the amount of satisfaction possible; comment on the nature of the human relationships in the job.

ii) Write a report on an evening course you've done in any subject.

7.5 Essay-writing

Model

Before you attempt to write an essay, you should be quite sure that you can write good, coherent paragraphs. If you want to practise writing paragraphs first, before you write an essay, work through Unit 7.1.

In a paragraph each piece of information contributes to the central theme of the paragraph. In an essay *each paragraph* contributes in some way to the development of the essay in one or other of the following ways:

A paragraph can
    present an argument or idea (1)
    present a counter or contrasting argument (2)
    illustrate an idea or argument (3)
    present facts or evidence (4)
    draw conclusions and summarise (5)
    offer comments on opinions or evidence (6)

The model essay on the next page, 'The Anglo-Saxon Disease' will investigate the function of the five paragraphs that make up the essay. Read the essay carefully and note how each paragraph contributes to the theme of the essay.

Linking
It is of course essential that an essay is clear, consistent, and logical; linking one idea/sentence to another one is therefore essential. Read the notes in the section 'Linking ideas' which follows the model essay to see how ideas are linked together in one piece of writing. There are many ways of linking ideas together:

i)   co-ordination (and, but, or)
ii)   words joining two complete parts of a sentence together (when, although, because, even if)
iii) replacement words (he, she; his, hers)
iv) pointer words (this, here, now; that, there, then)
v)   words that link a sentence to the one before it (therefore, secondly, on the other hand)
vi) word links (same word, synonym, opposite word or phrase)
vii) idea links (similar idea, contrasting idea)
viii) juxtaposition of facts (putting different facts next to each other)

When you write an essay make sure that each paragraph adds something to the essay, and each clause or sentence is linked effectively to something that has been written before it.

Read the essay below and the notes which follow:

THE ANGLO-SAXON DISEASE

Ⓐ

1 The study of strikes published today by the Department of Employment sets out to explode a myth, one which has greatly contributed over recent years to our decline in industrial confidence and in Britain's esteem

2 abroad. The myth is that the habit of going on strike is ingrained in our workforce, to an extent paralleled almost no-

3 where else. Like most myths, it is relatively easy to scotch by literalist methods, but much more difficult to demolish as

4 symbolic truth. Of course Britain is not unusual internationally, in terms of the number and

5 extent of its strikes: their effects are another matter. Ⓑ

6 The new study looks more closely than ever before at the strike record in manufacturing industry in three years (1971-73) which were intentionally chosen because they were especially

7 disturbed. In 1972, indeed, Britain must have been easily the most strike-ridden large nation

8 on earth; we lost about three times as many days per head of the workforce as in a normal

9 year. Nevertheless, the study shows that 95 per cent of factories were entirely free of strikes during the whole period.

10 Of the remainder only a third had more than one stoppage.

11 Even in parts of Britain notorious for bad labour relations all but a few factories were as peaceful

12 as those elsewhere. The same is apparently true (the figures are to appear later) of industries supposedly prone to unrest.

13 Although the study deals only with manufacturing industry, the picture it presents of general harmony and particular bitterness would be even more true

in the non-manufacturing sector, which includes the mines and the docks. Ⓒ

14 This is all well worth knowing. It sweeps away some exaggerated misconceptions and may help to overcome the reluctance of manufacturers to open plants in areas where militancy has frightened investment away. But it is not going to make "the English sickness" a meaningless concept. Exactly comparable figures for other countries may not exist, but no doubt they would also show only a tiny proportion of all workers engaging in serious strikes. Even in a bad year for earthquakes, one expects the ground to remain stable almost everywhere. Strikes never account for nearly as many days lost as illness and accidents, yet their economic significance is of a wholly different kind.

Ⓓ Britain usually ranks about fifth worst among major industrial nations in the table of days lost per head through strikes. Australia, Canada, Italy and the United States fairly regularly do worse ; indeed striking is something of an Anglo-Saxon disease. France generally loses fewer than half as many days, West Germany fewer than a tenth as many. Most comparable countries suffered an increase in unrest in the early 1970s, though Britain has enjoyed unusual peace in the last two years. The table of days lost does not by itself go far towards explaining Britain's economic decline.

Ⓔ What is not measured either by that table or by the new research is the damage that each strike does. In France and Italy many strikes are more in the nature of political feast-days—

⋙→

161

symbolic breaks for demonstrations that do not disrupt production unduly. In the United States strikes tend to be long and bitter, but also infrequent and predictable. Countries where each industry has one union are less subject than Britain to action by small groups bringing larger ones to a standstill. Britain has an usually high proportion of unofficial strikes. A method remains to be found of showing in figures how it is that British strikes hurt more, but the impression that they do is irresistible. The study does not show, and scarcely could, how many lost days strikes cause outside the plants where they occur, nor how many grievances ferment among workers laid off by other people's strikes—nor yet how much effect a strike may have on delivery times and export business. When all the misconceptions have been discounted and all allowance made for new laws on arbitration and workers' rights, neither managers nor trade unionists have anything to be complacent about in our disordered system of industrial relations.

Title: Fact and fiction about industrial strikes in Britain

Paragraphs

(A) Explains what the disease is (striking).
Explains what most people think about this ('the myth').
Reports that a Government study suggests different facts from those of the 'myth'.
(B) Reports factual contents of the report (1971–3).
(C) Comments on the significance of the evidence on the report.
(D) Presents more evidence on Britain's strikes, and makes comparisons with other countries.
(E) Presents a counter-argument to the report by suggesting some of the 'hidden' damaging effects of strikes.

Note The last sentence in the last paragraph is the main sentence of that paragraph, and possibly the main sentence of the whole essay.

Linking ideas

Below you will find an explanation of how the first 14 clauses/ideas are linked together. Go through this carefully, looking at the essay at the same time.

1	to 2:	lexical link	('myth' is repeated)
2	to 3:	lexical link	('myth' to 'like most myths')
3	to 4:	idea link	('easy to scotch by *literalist* methods' to 'of course Britain is not unusual ... in *number and extent* ...')
4	to 5:	lexical link	(contrast of '*number and extent* of its strikes' to '(the/their) *effects*' (of strikes))
5	to 6:	lexical link	(6 to 1 repetition of 'study')
		idea link	(5 to 6 'number/extent/effects' to 'strike record')

6	to 7:	sentence links	('indeed' expanding information in 6)
7	to 8:	idea links	(illustrating 7)
8	to 9:	conjunct and idea	('nevertheless' is a conjunct introducing a contrasting idea) (strike-ridden – free of strikes)
9	to 10:	lexical link or idea link	('95 per cent' to 'of the remainder')
10	to 11:	idea links	(more evidence for 10 and 9)
11	to 12:	same	('the same is true ...')
12	to 13:	NONE	(but link to 6 'manufacturing' and to rest of B)
13	to 14:	pointer word	('*this* is all well worth knowing ...' *This* really refers to 6–13)

Maybe you would like to analyse the rest of the essay for yourself.

WHAT TO DO

1 Make sure you understand the introductory paragraphs. If you don't, ask for further explanations from your teacher.
2 Read the essay called 'The Anglo-Saxon Disease'. Ask your teacher about anything you don't understand in the text.
   Then read the notes on paragraphs and linking ideas on page 162.
3 There are three linked practices in Unit 7.5, and it will be necessary to do these three practices one after the other.
   Practice 1 is about organising an essay in outline. When you and your teacher are happy that you can do this effectively move on to the next practice.
   Practice 2 is writing one of the essays you have planned in Practice 1. If you want more practice, simply use another of your previously planned essays from Practice 1.
   Practice 3 is planning and writing an essay on your own.
   There are no tests for this unit.

Practice 1

This first practice is designed just to start you thinking about writing an essay.

There are two essentials when writing an interesting essay:

1 The writer has something interesting to say and feels like saying it!
2 The writer is able to find the notional, linguistic and organisational forms to express what he wants to say.

This practice is about outline organisation of essays.

Below you will find ten essay topic areas, and two or three separate essay titles in each.

Chose *three* topic areas, then *one* essay from each area. You should have three essay titles then.

Music	1	'Most people listen to music to escape from something.'
	2	Write an essay on (a) Jazz (b) Rock, or (c) Folk Music.
Women	3	'Working women now have two jobs rather than just one.'
	4	Write an essay on the problems of being a woman in the last quarter of the twentieth century.
Men	5	Write an essay on a man you have admired or detested.
	6	'Men are finding it difficult to adjust to the demands of becoming more sensitive while still remaining masculine.'
Mind	7	'The average person is not very normal.' Discuss.
	8	Write an essay on the subject of depression.
Media	9	Write a critique of the press in your country.
	10	Which do you feel is the most reliable of the media and why: radio, TV, or newspapers?
Social issues	11	Write an essay on prisons.
	12	'In a compassionate, caring society, health and medicine would be entirely free.'
Politics	13	'I find politics so boring.' Discuss the reasons for this frequently-heard remark.
	14	Write on the subject 'Threats to world peace'.
Education	15	'Most of the time spent in school is completely wasted.'
	16	Discuss what qualities define the good *or* the bad teacher.
Relationships	17	Write an essay on one-parent families.
	18	'The trouble with modern marriages is that people don't try hard enough to make them work.' Discuss.
	19	'An open relationship is one in which one person doesn't want to possess the other.' Discuss.
Fashions	20	Write an essay on clothes fashions in the last five years.
	21	Discuss how you are affected by various fashions in dress and behaviour.

When you have chosen your three essays from the 21 listed above, spend 10 to 15 minutes writing down ideas on each essay as they come to you.

164

Now organise your ideas into four or five paragraphs (or more if you think this is necessary) so that you can present your ideas clearly and effectively. Here are some tips:

i) *Opening* paragraphs usually present the essay theme in outline, and suggest lines of development.
ii) The *final* paragraph tends to summarise the arguments, the evidence and the information in some way, and present tentative or clear (personal) conclusions.

Don't write your essay yet.

Below you will find an example of essay planning.

Essay theme: ETHICS

Essay title: Discuss the idea of honesty in your community.

Rough notes general belief in property (but Proudhon!?) – different
on ideas: sorts of theft (property, land, money, ideas) – punishments for theft not consistent – theft from employers and institutions regarded as normal – children as thieves – compulsive stealing (for love?) – taxes as state theft . . .

Paragraphs: 1 theft generally unacceptable, but some exceptions and paradoxes
2 stealing from individuals and consequent punishments
3 stealing from institutions, esp. employers – different from para 2
4 theft and social class – the class bias in Britain as seen in 'social benefit scrounging' v. tax-evasion
5 children – shoplifting – foreigners
6 conclusions – 'property is theft' (Proudhon) – no absolute moral standards adhered to. Most people inconsistent because 'possession' difficult to justify.

Your teacher will mark your essay plans. DO NOT throw them away – you will need them for Practice 2.

Practice 2

Practice 1 in this unit was the preparation for this practice. So in order to do this practice you need your work (which should have been marked) from Practice 1.

For Practice 2 you should take *one* of the essays you prepared in outline paragraph form and write a fully-expanded essay, (perhaps somewhere between 350 and 600 words, but it depends how much you have to say).

Remember what was written before the model essay about *linking* devices.

Practice 3

In this practice your teacher does not want to see the mechanics of your essay-writing, so you needn't show him/her the notes and essay-plan.

However, planning and organisation will still be important before you start, even if you develop away from your plan as you write.

Choose one of the topic areas below.
Suggest a theme to yourself, or work from one of those given.
Plan your essay.
Write your essay.
Read your essay back to yourself and check that it reads well, and makes good, interesting sense.

Suggested themes:
1 Arts   (popular music / museums dead? / opera / the cinema)
2 Women/Men (sexual equality / having children / marriage for ever?)
3 Education (language learning / private education / boredom at school)
4 Britain   (the dying island / friendly and reserved / Britain and Europe)
5 People   (modern friendship / mobility and the loss of local life)
6 Religion   (and today / many gods / as an escape)
7 Sport   (sport and politics / professionalism)
8 Crime   (explanations of / crime and punishment)
9 Feelings   (nostalgia / jealousy and envy / experience of terror)
10 Work   (work and play / just rewards / unemployment)

166

Acknowledgements

The author and publishers are grateful to the authors, publishers and others who have given permission for the use of copyright material identified in the text. It has not been possible to identify the sources of all the material used and in such cases the publishers would welcome information from copyright owners.

Sylvester Jacobs for the photograph on page 59; John Walmsley for the photographs on pages 59 and 73; *Radio Times* for the photograph on page 60; Department for National Savings and Dorland Advertising Ltd for the drawings by Paul Sample on pages 68 and 69; South Devon Technical College, Art Department for the prints on pages 73 and 74; Sally and Richard Greenhill, Photographers Photo Library for the photograph on page 74; *Sunday Express* for the article on page 89; Geraldine Stoneham for the short story on page 90; Stafford-Miller Ltd for the advertisement on page 100; Oxfam, Webb Ivory Ltd, J. D. Williams Group Ltd for the advertisements on page 106; The Royal Society for the Protection of Birds for the advertisement on page 107; The Peter Jones Collection for the advertisement on page 108; Halifax Building Society for the advertisement on page 109; Ansvar Insurance Company Ltd for the advertisement on page 110; National Westminster Bank PLC for the advertisement on page 111; Abbey National Building Society for the advertisement on page 123; The National Film and Television School for the advertisement on page 124; Mr Peter Keen and British Railways Board for the letter on page 142; Mr Frank Heller and The Tavistock Institute of Human Relations for the letter on page 146; Philip Youd & Irving for the advertisement on page 150; *The Guardian* for the article on page 151; Syndication International Ltd for the letter on page 152; Times Newspapers Ltd for the article on page 161.

Book design by Peter Ducker MSTD
Drawings by Chris Evans (pages 63 and 65), Reg Piggott (pages 95 and 96) and Trevor Ridley (pages 84, 85, 92, 93 and 94).